IF IT RUNS

BREAST CANCER

REDUCING YOUR RISK

IF IT RUNS IN YOUR FAMILY

BREAST CANCER

REDUCING YOUR RISK

Mary Dan Eades, M.D.

Foreword by A. Toth, M.D.

Developed by the Philip Lief Group, Inc.

A
BANTAM
TRADE
PAPERBACK

BANTAM BOOKS
NEW YORK · TORONTO · LONDON · SYDNEY · AUCKLAND

This book is not intended as a substitute for the medical advice of physicians. The reader should regularly consult a physician in matters relating to his or her health and particularly with respect to any symptoms which may require diagnosis or medical attention. Readers should also speak with their own doctors about their individual needs before starting any diet or fitness program. Consulting one's personal physician about diet and exercise is especially important if the reader is on any medication or is already under medical care for any illness.

IF IT RUNS IN YOUR FAMILY: BREAST CANCER
A Bantam Book / April 1991

All rights reserved.
Copyright © 1991 by The Philip Lief Group, Inc.
Cover art copyright © 1991 by Eye Tooth Design.
Book design by GDS / Jeffrey L. Ward

Library of Congress Cataloging-in-Publication Data
Eades, Mary Dan.
   If it runs in your family : breast cancer : reducing your risk /
by Mary Dan Eades ; reviewed and with a foreword by A. Toth.
      p.   cm.
Includes bibliographical references.
ISBN 0-553-34953-8
1. Breast—Cancer—Risk factors.   2. Breast—Cancer—Popular
works.   I. Toth, A.   II. Title.
RC280.B8E2   1991
616.99'449—dc20   90-45180
                                                              CIP
Published simultaneously in the United States and Canada

PRINTED IN THE UNITED STATES OF AMERICA

OPM   0 9 8 7 6 5 4 3 2 1

092994

For Mike
my husband, my best friend, my colleague

Acknowledgments

My thanks to Alan Mahony of the Philip Lief Group for his editorial help and to my friends and editors Cathy Hemming and the late Jamie Rothstein for choosing me to write this project. They have all been unfailingly helpful and patient in their editorial direction.

I also appreciate the information and help given me by my friends and colleagues, Dr. David Harshfield and Dr. Joseph M. Beck III, on the radiology and oncology portions of this book, and by my sister, Rose Crane, for directing me to the resources for guided imagery. Thanks also go to Lisa Wooten for her help on illustrations at a moment's notice, and to Sarah Herring Graves for her help in running down procedure codes and costs.

Thanks, finally, to my staff, friends, and my very patient and long-suffering children—Ted, Daniel, and Scott—for understanding the time commitment required to bring this project together.

Contents

Foreword

As a practicing gynecologist, I've come to realize over the years that the prospect of having breast cancer frightens women more than the possibility of any other kind of cancer. In response, I've tried to impress upon my patients the importance of early detection in curing this pernicious disease. Now that Dr. Mary Dan Eades has written this book, an even wider audience can benefit from that message, along with other lifesaving advice as well.

Dr. Eades explains the risk factors every woman should be aware of. By far, heredity plays the largest part in determining an individual's risk. And in this book, women can help determine their chances of developing a tumor by charting a few simple facts about their family history on the genogram Dr. Eades offers. It has a simple, straightforward approach.

By following Dr. Eades's advice and setting up a regular program of self-examination, women at risk can greatly improve their chances for survival and gain peace of mind. Routine physician's examinations, along with mammograms and a sensible attitude toward diet and exercise form a foundation for a lifetime of health.

In addition to Dr. Eades's wise suggestions, this book also explores the different kinds of breast cancer that can develop, as well as the various forms of treatment available. Readers will be surprised to note that in certain cases drug therapy programs are preferred over surgery.

Researchers have made many advances in combating breast cancer. Dr. Eades's book discusses the new frontiers medicine has reached with drugs such as interferon, as well as startling developments with image therapy and antibody cloning.

But the most encouraging news that Dr. Eades offers—and that I strongly agree with—is that early detection works. You have the power to save and protect your life. More than that, you can help save the lives of your mother, your sister—even your daughters. You owe it to them, and to yourself, to read this book.

A. TOTH, M.D.
The New York Hospital—Cornell Medical Center

Introduction

When I was approached to write this book, I began sorting through the mountain of research that has been done on breast cancer. I wanted to give my readers definite answers to the question of what puts them at risk for breast cancer, and I reasoned that if I distilled all the research down far enough, those answers would be apparent. In some cases, a clear answer did emerge, but in most cases—especially in regard to the environmental risk factors—the deeper I delved into the very latest research, the less black and white the findings became.

I can certainly understand your wanting this book to give you definitive answers about your risk for breast cancer. However, what I must impress on you is this: Breast cancer is an immensely complex disease with many external factors contributing to its development or promoting its growth once established. Because of the complex interplay of environment and heredity, there is no single straightforward explanation as to its cause. And because I often found evidence supporting both sides of many issues, I decided to present the consensus view.

You will also notice that throughout this book, I have made reference to breast cancer as though it were a disease exclusive to women, and, of course, it is not. Men do develop breast cancer, but very rarely, and most of the risk factors that apply to women apply to men as well. I trust that the men among my readers will understand my decision to use the feminine designation. Constantly having to refer to "man or woman," "he or she," "his or her" would have been unwieldy for both the reader and the writer.

Whether you are a man or a woman, a person concerned about your own risk for breast cancer or that of someone you love, this book will offer you several things: a clearer insight into both the genetic and environmental causes for breast cancer, a means to determine your personal risk as well as that of your loved ones, some commonsense medical advice about health and nutrition as they relate to preventing breast cancer, a demystification of the available medical and surgical treatment of the disease for those of you who may wish to know more about them, and a message of hope through an examination of the current research that may change the face of this disease for future generations.

I hope that after reading this book, you will come away with a greater understanding both of what it means to be at risk for breast cancer and what you can do to reduce that risk.

1

What It Means to Be at Risk

We interrupt our regularly scheduled program to bring you this important news bulletin. The local police have just announced that a resident has spotted the infamous serial killer who recently escaped from the state penitentiary. He was last seen on Elm Street in the Heights area of our city. His murders have generally followed the same pattern with rare exceptions; his victims have been Caucasian women, more than forty years old, who have red hair and wear glasses. All of the victims own or drive blue station wagons. The police have urged all women fitting this description to take the strictest precautions and to report any suspicious individuals immediately.

*   *   *

What if driving down the street one evening, you heard this announcement on your car radio? Would it grab your attention? Would it be of serious importance to you? Perhaps not, if you happened to be a twenty-year-old black man who drives a red sedan or a thirty-five-year-old blond who drives a green corvette. But what if you happened to be a forty-three-year-old woman? The announcement holds a little more importance. And what if you have reddish hair or wear glasses? Even more important. And what if you're turning into your driveway at 138 Elm Street in your baby blue Volvo station wagon when you hear this announcement?

The woman in this scenario has the great misfortune of having multiple *risk factors,* which make her selection by the killer more likely. Some of these factors she can control or change, some she cannot; but the more information she has about what puts her at risk, the more of these risk factors she can eliminate, and the less likely the killer will be to strike her. And, of course, she would be foolish not to try to alter as many of her risk factors as possible. She may dye her hair, get contact lenses, and take public transportation, although she can do nothing about her age or race.

As a physician with a busy general family practice, I frequently see women confronting very similar problems, as do other physicians all across America. These women fit the description— because of their age, sex, race, family history, diet, and habits— and, consequently, have a greater risk for being selected as the next victim of an ancient serial killer: breast cancer.

Perhaps that woman is you, your mother, sister, aunt, or daughter, or perhaps all five. If so, then reading this book will help you to identify and better understand those factors that put women at greater risk for developing this disease, as well as the steps they can take to reduce that risk. Remember, being at risk only means the killer likes your type; he hasn't caught you until he's caught you. Your chances of eluding his grasp improve dramatically if you know what he's looking for.

Do You Fit the General Description?

In the United States, 1 out of every 11 women will develop breast cancer, and every year, nearly 40,000 of these women will die from their disease. It is the leading cancer killer among women—a lead that is being challenged by lung cancer thanks to the rising number of women smokers. This year alone, physicians like me will tell more than 130,000 American women that their breast lump is a cancer. Who are these women? What is it about them that puts them at risk?

In general demographic terms, breast cancer strikes

- *Women far more often than men.* We generally think of breast cancer as a female disease, and indeed it is 100 times more common in women. Men, however, have not escaped the disease entirely, and their cancer prognosis tends not to be as good when they *do* develop it.
- *Caucasians more often than blacks.* This demographic statistic is slightly misleading, because while most studies do show a slightly higher rate of breast cancer diagnosis among Caucasian women than black women, a greater percentage of the black population dies from their disease. Several theories have been postulated as to why this should be the case, and although there may certainly be some variation on a genetic or ethnic basis as to the kind of breast cancer that develops, primarily social factors seem to be at work. A higher level of awareness of the disease and greater access to medical resources brings more Caucasian women to di-

agnosis and treatment earlier in their illness and, therefore, at a more curable stage.

• *More commonly after age fifty.* The diagnosis of breast cancer before the age of twenty is quite rare indeed. The disease, while present in slightly greater numbers in the thirties, becomes the most common cause of death among women between forty and forty-five, and the incidence begins to climb even more sharply after the age of fifty-five.

• *Obese people more than thin ones.* Older women—those past menopause in particular—assume a greater risk for breast cancer if they carry an excess of body fat. Medical researchers believe this phenomenon may occur in part because female hormone precursors of estrogen are activated in fatty tissue. The greater above ideal a woman's body fat percentage, the more of this kind of estrogen hormone she makes and *stores* in the fatty tissue to be slowly released over time. Older women also seem to have breast tumors that are more sensitive to hormonal stimulation. Their increased body fat—and consequently elevated estrogen levels—may place them at higher risk; hormones seem to play an important role in causing breast cancer.

• *Smokers slightly more than nonsmokers.* Although many fine studies over the years have failed to prove that cigarette smoking promotes breast cancer, several recent studies have shown a correlation between cigarette smoking and the development of breast cancer (along with the known association of smoking with cancers of the lung, oral cavity, larynx, esophagus, and cervix). But the issue still remains a cloudy one because one study—which received a fair amount of play in the lay press—went so far as to demonstrate a slight reduction in breast cancer rates among smokers. Although such a finding no doubt pleased the smoking population and the tobacco-producing industries, all other studies I have seen demonstrate a causative or promoting role for smoking and breast cancer—some showing a stronger correlation than others.

• *More commonly in Western cultures.* While breast cancer has for years been the most common malignant disease among women in the Western world, the occurrence rates among certain non-Western women—for reasons that have yet to be clearly defined—are quite low. Studies of Japanese women have revealed a particularly low rate of incidence. The rates for Japanese women do increase when they migrate to Western cultures, so clearly more than an inherited resistance to the development of the disease must be considered. The women of Hawaii suffer much higher rates of occurrence than many Western countries, although at least a portion of their gene pool arose from Japan. However, the rates in Hawaii are not as high as those in the rest of the United States, or in England, Ireland, Israel, and the Netherlands, where women have the highest rates of breast cancer of all countries in the world.

Many studies have been conducted to determine how much these ethnic differences can be attributed to genetics and heredity and the extent to which diet and other environmental factors play a role. The consensus of the research seems to be that while both heredity and environment have an impact on breast cancer development, those cancers that occur before menopause have a stronger genetic basis, and those occurring later in life result more from environmental influences.

Profile of the Woman at Risk:
The Five Key Traits

Within all ethnic categories and age groups, however, medical researchers have consistently identified five common characteristics in women who develop breast cancer.

You should consider yourself (and/or your family members or loved ones) at higher risk for developing breast cancer if:

1. You have a first-degree relative (mother or sister) who had breast cancer.
2. You have a previous history of breast cancer in one breast already or a history of a certain type of benign breast disease (called proliferative disease with atypia, which I will discuss more fully in chapter 5).
3. You have never given birth to a child and have passed the age at which you could.
4. You were more than thirty years old at the time of your first pregnancy.
5. You began menstruation at an early age (before age twelve) or entered menopause late (after age fifty-five).

Women with all five of these particular risk factors develop breast cancer at a rate *at least three to four times higher than the normal population.* But even if the genetic cards have been stacked against her—even though she may have no control over her family history—a woman at risk for developing breast cancer should not despair. There are many things she can do to lower her risk dramatically. A disease such as breast cancer arises from multiple causes with both environmental and hereditary influences playing important roles. In this book, we will examine the various environmental causes, such as diet, alcohol consumption, smoking, and hormones, as well as the evidence that points to an inherited tendency for development of the disease. Let's begin with the latter.

2

The Genetic Factors

Self-Test

Please answer the following questions before reading on.

• Did your mother develop breast cancer (if so, note if her cancer involved one breast or both, and if it occurred before or after menopause. If it developed in both breasts before menopause, your risk is higher.)?

• Do you have any male relatives with breast cancer?

• Has breast cancer occured on your father's side of the family, such as in his mother or his sisters?

• Do you have a sister who has had breast cancer (if so, note if her cancer involved one breast or both, and if it occurred before or after menopause)?

- Did either of your grandmothers suffer breast cancer?
- Have you already had a breast cancer yourself?
- Has cancer of the colon occurred frequently in your family?
- Has cancer of the ovary occurred frequently in your family?

A yes answer to any of these questions indicates you may have a family history that puts you at risk for breast cancer, and you will want to pay careful attention to the following information about the genetic causes of breast cancer. The greater the number of yes answers, the more likely it is that your family carries genes that may put you at increased risk. Remember, however, that just being at risk does *not* mean you *will* develop breast cancer. It only means that you must be more vigilant about prevention and all the more careful to eliminate or control as many external environmental risk factors as you can.

If, on the other hand, you have answered no to all of these questions, your inherited risk for breast cancer is low. Although your lifestyle may increase your risk somewhat—and you should still read about these environmental risk factors in chapter 3 to determine if you have them—you are fortunate that the genetic cards stack up in your favor.

Genetics, Genes, and Chromosomes: How We Become What We Are

Whether you're tall or short, blond or brunet, have blue eyes or green ones, you inherited those traits from your parents. Maybe you got your curly red hair and freckles from your father, or your dimpled chin from Grampa Joe, or perhaps everyone tells you it's amazing how much you look like your mom. Certainly, we recognize that these kinds of heritable traits pass from parent to child. But how does this occur? Through chemical messages stored in our chromosomes. These genetic messengers are like carefully wound-up computer programs, only on a submicroscopic scale. Let me explain briefly for those readers who may not be totally familiar with the concept of chromosomes and inheritance, because this information will be essential to understanding the genetics of breast cancer.

If we go all the way back to the moment of our conception, an egg cell, or ovum, carrying twenty-three of these chromosomes contributed by our mother, combines with a sperm cell, carrying twenty-three chromosomes contributed from our father. The newly formed cell created by the union of the egg and the sperm, we call a *zygote*. The single-celled zygote, now with a complete set of forty-six chromosomes, contains every bit of the preprogrammed chemical (genetic) information needed to develop a whole new human being, different from all others. As the zygote divides to make two cells, and those two divide to make four, and so on, the set of chromosomes duplicates and reduplicates with each division, so that the messages on the original forty-six chromosomes pass to each and every one of the cells in the developing embryo.

The chromosomes themselves are made up of strands of DNA (deoxyribonucleic acid), which in turn is made up of millions and millions of subunits called bases, or base pairs. The bases function much like Morse code signals in that they are "read" in a specific order; the order determines an encoded message meaningful to anyone capable of understanding the code.

A gene, on the other hand, is but a grouping of these bases (maybe 40,000 or 50,000 of them per gene) in a specific location along a chromosome strand that contains the codes of a particular message. The message, for example, may be to make a special protein that makes the eyes brown or the hair black, or stimulates greater growth for a longer period of time to make us tall, or causes the cells of the nose cartilage to develop a certain way, giving it a shape similar to our mother's or father's.

However, much more than simply our appearance comes to us through our genes. We may also inherit Uncle Jim's pollen allergies or Grandad's flat feet, for example, or health problems of a more serious nature—such as heart disease, diabetes, and high blood pressure, and yes, a tendency for developing breast cancer.

But I must again remind you that in regard to breast cancer, genetic factors are far from the only explanation. Simply being passed a gene or group of genes that *may* under the right stimulus result in breast cancer is a far cry from inheriting a gene that *causes* breast cancer. It's much like a game of cards: the hand you're dealt may not count as much as how you choose to play it.

An enormous amount of research into which particular genes might be in part responsible for breast cancer has already led researchers to the discovery of some specific areas on several chromosomes. Careful study of these genes will ultimately lead to the discovery of genetic markers. These markers will allow physicians and genetics specialists to identify with accuracy whether a woman is at higher risk for a disease by studying samples of her blood or tissue. This technique, which we will discuss in more depth a little later on, is already in use for several other diseases.

Where Do You Fall on the Genetic Ladder?

Genealogy, the tracing of your family's roots, enjoyed a great resurgence a few years back thanks to Alex Haley's blockbuster novel *Roots* and the television miniseries that followed it. Perhaps in response you dabbled in finding out about your family's history, maybe even tracing your lineage back to a great-great-great-grand-someone. What you probably did not do, however—because such information is rarely shared—was to take note of what ailments your earlier ancestors suffered or died from. This kind of information, which I encourage all of you to begin to search for, can help you and your family live longer, wiser, and perhaps healthier lives than your forebears. Luckily, those relatives most important in assessing your risk for developing any heritable disease may still be living, and so information about this nearest branch of the family tree is hopefully readily available to you.

Where to Begin Your Search

Because research teams have repeatedly established that a greater risk for developing breast cancer exists in first-degree relatives of breast cancer victims, I urge that you begin here. Your *first-degree relatives* are your mother (and father), your full-blood sisters (and brothers), and your daughters (and sons). You can begin to get an idea of your own inherited risk for breast cancer by tracing the disease along the branches of your family tree, starting with yourself.

In constructing a family *genogram* in regard to your own risk of breast cancer, include these closest relatives—your sisters, mother, aunts, and your grandmothers on both sides of your family. Although the disease does not occur frequently in men, if you should have a male relative (whether father, grandfather, uncle, or brother) who had breast cancer, be certain to include him, too. If you wish to identify your own daughter's risk of inheriting breast cancer, you might want to do a separate genogram that includes your husband's side of the family as well—

his mother, grandmothers, and sisters and any male relatives who might have had breast cancer.

In preparing the skeleton of your family tree, you can use the standard genogram symbols recommended by the Task Force of the North American Primary Care Research Group and described in *Genograms in Family Assessment* by Monica Mc-Goldrick and Randy Gerson (W. W. Norton & Co, 1985). Or you can invent any symbols you like—as long as you distinguish between female and male family members and between those still alive and those who have died. The standard genogram symbols are

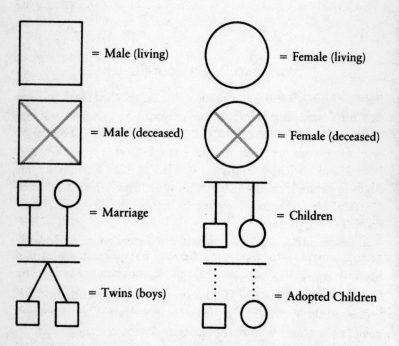

Although not all of these symbols will be used for your genogram, they will be helpful should you wish to construct genograms to track various other aspects of your family's medical history.

In addition to these basic symbols, you may want to draw a double line around your own symbol to distinguish yourself from the rest of your family. Fill in everyone's name and year of birth, as well as the year of death for anyone who has died. When you have finished drawing the skeleton of your family tree, you will have a diagram that resembles Figure 1. Once you have this skeleton, you can begin adding the specific notes that will help you trace your family history of breast cancer or other related cancers.

Be as thorough as you can in writing down—next to each person's symbol—what you readily know about the occurrence of breast cancer among these relatives, which may be quite a lot or very little. Include whether the relative developed cancer in both breasts or one, the time in life (before or after menopause) when the breast cancer developed, and what risk factors she had, as Figure 2. demonstrates.

The presence of other kinds of cancers may be relevant to your genogram, so be sure to take careful note of them. Sometimes cancer syndromes occur that involve the breast and other organs, such as ovary, thyroid gland, colon, brain, lungs, blood, and adrenal gland. Cancer syndromes are inherited groups of different but related cancers that occur within a family group. While one family member may have multiple types of these related cancers—for example, she may have breast cancer *and* thyroid cancer, or breast cancer *and* ovarian cancer—what you will probably most often see, is one family member with breast cancer, another with ovarian cancer, another with thyroid cancer, etc.

The presence of other cancers in your family may indicate that you are at higher risk of breast cancer. The genograms will help you pick out a pattern of cancer occurrence that you may not

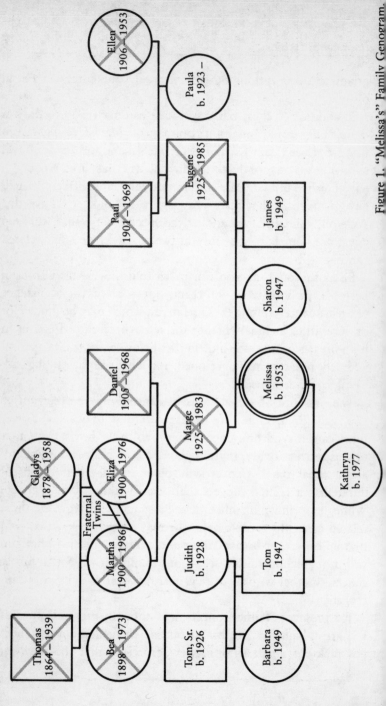

Figure 1. "Melissa's" Family Genogram.

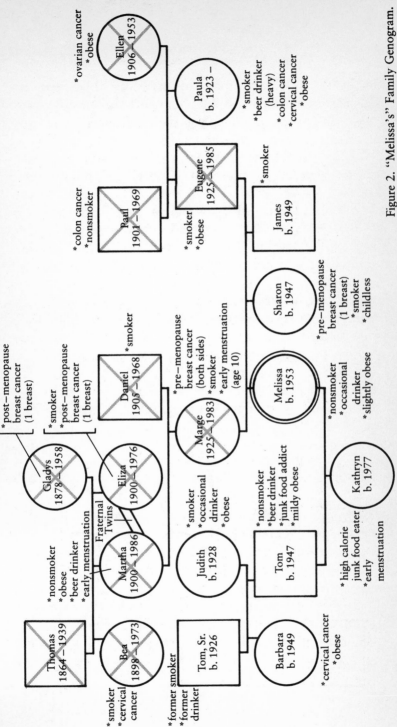

Figure 2. "Melissa's" Family Genogram.

have ever recognized before, but that could be important additional information in assessing your breast cancer risk. If these other cancers appear among your family members (male or female), note them as well. Although there may be some variation in which type of cancer occurs, the cancer syndrome passes directly to each generation through a single gene from parent to child.

Don't be discouraged if you cannot complete the genogram right away. As you read through this and the subsequent chapters and gain a clearer understanding of the disease and its various risk factors, you can return to the chart and fill in any new information.

Also, you may have noted on the family genogram that I have listed habits, such as smoking, high-calorie diet, alcohol use, and junk-food addiction, whether or not the relative suffered from obesity, has had children, or menstruated early. These are examples of the environmental risk factors that you will learn about in chapter 3. Your family's bad habits will not put you at risk, but if you have any of these habits you may be at higher risk.

A Short Course in Genetic Transmission

Before you can interpret your family genogram, you need to know a little about the genetic transmission of cancer. As I have already said, we receive one-half of our genetic information—our genes—from our mother and the other half from our father.

The end product of the genetic message—called the *expression* of the gene—results in the traits we see (such as blue eyes, dark skin, or tall stature). The passage and expression of our genes can be predicted by following set rules of genetic inheritance. We call these rules Mendelian inheritance in honor of Gregor

Mendel, a monk who traced and recorded the basic truths of dominant and recessive genetic transmission by studying the traits of peas, which he tended in the monastery garden. He noticed that by cross-pollinating his pea plants in a controlled fashion, he could tell from the parent plants' traits what the seedling plants would look like. By keeping careful records, he developed mathematical rules to predict what the offspring of two parents would yield, what traits would always be expressed (*dominant traits*), and which ones would only be expressed if both parents passed the trait on to the next generation (*recessive traits*). Although these Mendelian rules do not apply to all cases of inheritance, they form the basis for medical genetics and are fundamental to our understanding of the genetics of breast cancer. Let me illustrate these rules with a short example.

At the simplest level, we will assume that a single gene pair controls each trait, although in many cases, expression of a trait depends on the interplay and contribution of multiple gene pairs. Let's use as our hypothetical example the fur color of a cat, and let's assume that the fur can only be white or black. Let's say that the gene for black fur is the dominant gene—meaning that it will always be expressed if it is present, and the cat who carries this gene will be a black cat. White fur, then, will be our recessive trait. We want to mate a white female cat with a black male cat and predict the fur color of the kittens.

To keep it simple, we must begin with pure strains, meaning that the black-furred cat has both his genes as dominant genes for black fur (which we will designate *B* and *B*), and the white-furred parent has two recessive genes for white fur (which we will designate *b* and *b*, using the lower case to represent the recessive form of the fur color gene).

We now cross our parent black cat with his white mate:

BB-------bb

The parents, you remember, will each donate one of their two genes for fur color to each of their kittens as follows:

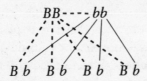

Because we began with pure-bred black and white cats, the black cat, which we have called the male, could only donate dominant *B* genes, since that is all he had. The same is true for the pure-bred white mother cat, she could only donate recessive *b* genes to her kittens, because that's all she had to give. Their litter of four kittens will *all* be black, although each of them is a hybrid— that is, each kitten carries one dominant *B* gene from its father and one recessive *b* gene from its mother. But because *B* is a dominant gene, it will be expressed in any individual who has it; therefore, all the kittens will have black fur.

In the next generation, things can get a little more interesting, so let's now mate two kittens out of this all-black hybrid litter. These black-furred parents will have fur color genes like this:

$$Bb ---- Bb$$

Again, each parent will donate one or the other of its two genes to each of its kittens. If we again have four kittens from this crossing of cats, we might get any of the following combinations:

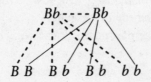

In this litter, three of the kittens will be black, but if the genes did align as I have shown one will have white fur. It is possible that the random shuffling of the genes could result in *no* white kittens as well. I do not intend to imply it *must* occur.

Like fur color in our cat example, the cancer syndrome in humans passes from generation to generation genetically. The vast majority of inherited cancers, however, do not obey so simple a scheme. The human genome (the complete set of all genes in an individual) is infinitely more complex, with millions of genes controlling millions of traits, but the same basic truths apply. And, for practical purposes, this is the mechanism by which all traits pass from one generation to the next.

This very simple scenario should also help explain from a genetic standpoint why you may sometimes see a particular trait skip generations, or be expressed in one child but not in others. It also points out the importance of tracing your genogram back a few generations if you can.

The Search for Proof of a Genetic Cause for Breast Cancer

Since the time of Galen, the ancient Greek physician, medical scientists studying breast cancer have been aware that a woman afflicted with this disease often had one or more close relatives who had previously developed it as well, very often a first-degree relative—in particular, her mother or sister. Modern cancer researchers have now begun to look for some pattern, marker, or change in specific genes that could be used by physicians to identify those women most at risk more closely.

But what will this information, once found, mean to patients at risk? To what degree are diseases, such as breast cancer, the result of genetic factors? The basic question of inheritance versus environment has always plagued scientists searching for the cause of familial diseases. And, unfortunately, this question does not have an easy answer. Families often share more than their genes; they frequently have similar eating and social habits and live in similar environmental settings. To settle the issue of environment versus inheritance, genetic researchers must turn to an age-old method, nature's perfect genetic laboratory: the study of the disease in twins.

What Do Twin Studies Tell Us?

Twins come, of course, in two types: *identical twins* who share not only the same womb, but also the same set of genes, as a result of having come from the same fertilized egg, and *fraternal twins* who are wombmates during the nine months of pregnancy, but come from two separate eggs. Fraternal twins share no greater genetic likeness than other brothers and sisters.

By studying the occurrence of a disease in both kinds of twins, researchers can determine if that disease results primarily from inheritance or environment. For example, if genetic factors alone cause breast cancer, then both identical twins with a genetic history of breast cancer should most often (virtually always) develop the disease. Fraternal twins, on the other hand, should develop breast cancer more often than the general population (because they do have more genes in common than strangers) but no more often than sisters who are not twins. If environmental factors alone cause the disease, then we should expect to find breast cancer no more often in identical twins than in fraternal twins or other sisters, or even nonrelated individuals living in the same environment, who have similar dietary and social habits.

Breast Cancer Twin Study Results

Dr. Niels Holm and his colleagues in Denmark conducted a study of the occurrence of breast cancers in twins. Their extensive evaluation, published in 1980, relied on information available in the Danish Twin Register.* (This invaluable source contains a full medical history from birth to death of about 6,000 pairs of twins born in Denmark between 1870 and 1920.)

The results of this study showed that if breast cancer developed in one of a pair of identical twins, the other twin developed the disease six times more often than she would have had she not been the twin. In fraternal twins, if one twin suffered breast cancer, the other twin was two times more likely to develop the disease. These findings certainly support the theory for a genetic role in the development of breast cancer. But they do not give us a neat-and-tidy answer to the genetics versus environment question, because all studies on twins have not shown as clear a difference.

Although about 8 to 9 percent of breast cancers do seem to pass from parent to child via a single dominant gene (based on the occurrence rates among twins), most breast cancers do not seem to be passed on in accordance with the simple rules of genetics that were developed by Father Mendel.

Geneticists and physicians do recognize this kind of straightforward transmission in many inherited physical traits and diseases such as baldness, hemophilia, cystic fibrosis, sickle cell anemia, and the ABO blood types. The presence or absence of one gene in these instances determines the onset of the disease.

Instead of this simple mode of inheritance, the development of more than 90 percent of breast cancers most likely occurs

*Holm, N.V. et al., "Etiologic Factors of Breast Cancer Elucidated by a Study of Unselected Twins," *Journal of National Cancer Institute.* Vol. 65 No. 2, pp. 285–297. August 1980.

from multiple genes at several spots on several different chromosomes. To complicate matters further, just because a woman carries the genes that could be a cause of some kinds of breast cancer, she won't necessarily develop the disease. Exposure to certain environmental factors may have to occur before the genes will express themselves in the development of breast cancer. This mode of genetic passage—which is not peculiar to breast cancer but is seen in many other cancers and diseases—makes it much more difficult to predict who will develop the disease. And so the issue of a specific genetic basis for breast cancer remains unclear, implying we may be able to combat a genetic predisposition to the disease by controlling environmental factors.

Why the Confusion?

The muddying of the waters in the search for a clear-cut genetic origin for breast cancer has occurred at least in part because for many years physicians and medical researchers approached breast cancer as though it were a single disease. Breast cancer is breast cancer, right? Wrong.

There seem to be at least two distinct kinds of breast cancer, which behave very differently in their presentation, aggression, and response to treatment, and which more than likely result from different genetic malfunctions.

The breast cancer that develops earlier in life—before menopause—tends to be more aggressive (faster growing and quicker to spread, or metastasize, to other areas). It arises more often in both breasts or in multiple sites within the same breast instead of as a single tumor in one breast, and it does not seem to respond as well to treatment with the new antiestrogen drugs (such as Tamoxifen).

The majority of cases of breast cancer, however, arise in women past the time of menopause. These cancers usually occur as a single tumor in one breast, grow more slowly, metastasize later in their course, and often respond quite well to treatment with Tamoxifen and other antiestrogen drugs. We will discuss the particulars of the various kinds of breast cancers in chapter 5 and their modes of treatment in chapter 6. But at this point, let's take a look at the differences in breast cancer risk in relatives of women with these two distinct kinds of cancer.

The Early Developing Breast Cancers and Family Risk

The kind of breast cancer that develops early—typically between the late thirties and midforties—behaves quite differently, from a medical point of view, from the disease that arises in women in their late fifties, sixties, and seventies. Physicians and cancer researchers now make the distinction between *premenopausal* and *postmenopausal* breast cancers, because although they both arise as cancers in the breast tissue, that's where their similarities end.

From an inherited risk standpoint, a family history for premenopausal cancer is of substantially greater importance than one for later-life breast cancer. Genetic factors seem to be more clearly at work in the development of the early cancers.

Virtually all the scientific research on breast cancer that has been published in the last twenty years has supported the medical notion that, generally speaking, the daughters and sisters of early breast cancer patients are at significantly greater risk for the disease than the population as a whole. The extent of that risk varies from study to study, but several well-conducted studies estimate the increase in risk at from three to nine times higher than the general population. Most studies agree that:

- DAUGHTERS AND SISTERS OF PREMENOPAUSAL BREAST CANCER PATIENTS HAVE A FIVE TO SIX TIMES GREATER RISK OF DEVELOPING THE DISEASE.
- IN CASES IN WHICH THE CANCER INVOLVES BOTH BREASTS, THE RISK FOR DAUGHTERS AND SISTERS INCREASES TO NINE TIMES GREATER.

However, one study showed that relatives of some women whose disease falls within the broad heading of premenopausal breast cancer suffer an even greater and more startling risk.

This work—done in the early 1970s by David E. Anderson, Ph.D., at the University of Texas Cancer Center in Houston— identified a group of very high risk women among the relatives of certain breast cancer patients. What features set these women apart? What description did they fit that put them at an incredible forty-seven to fifty-one times greater risk than normal? These ultrahigh risk women were the *sisters* of premenopausal breast cancer patients whose mothers had also developed early breast cancer, often in both breasts.

This excellent study allows physicians to identify a group of women who, because their family history places them at a much increased risk, need especially careful screening and regular follow-up. To state it another way,

- THE STRONGEST FAMILY RISK OF ALL OCCURS IN WOMEN WHO HAVE A FAMILY HISTORY OF PREMENOPAUSAL BREAST CANCER IN *BOTH* THEIR MOTHER AND A FULL-BLOOD SISTER. THESE WOMEN HAVE A RISK FIFTY TIMES GREATER THAN THOSE WOMEN WITHOUT A FAMILY HISTORY OF DEVELOPING THE DISEASE.

These women, like our redheaded woman in the blue station wagon, have the misfortune to have genes that make them an easier and more likely target for breast cancer. And like our redhead, these women must work extra hard to eliminate environmental risk factors over which they *do* have control in an effort to reduce their risk (see chapter 3). Despite the higher risk they face, women with family histories of premenopausal breast cancer can benefit a great deal from these efforts.

In this scenario, the disease probably would result from the passage of a single gene from parent to child, and this may cause potential parents some concern.

It is not unheard of for women who fall into very high risk groups for any disease to become so frightened of passing the disease on to a child that they avoid becoming a parent. This decision, while in many ways understandable, turns a genetic risk into a life-long tragedy, and an unnecessary one. In the case of breast cancer, not bearing children actually increases a woman's risk of contracting the disease. And again, although the genetic message may pass to a child, this doesn't mean the cancer will inevitably follow. It simply requires that all family members be more vigilant about their lifestyle and habits, and take extra care to be screened frequently, so that if the disease does arise, it can be caught early, at a more curable stage.

As I have stated, premenopausal and postmenopausal breast cancer should be considered two different diseases. If you are at risk for one of them you are not necessarily at risk for the other. If you are a woman past menopause who has premenopausal breast cancer in your family, although you should still be on your guard, your risk is probably not as great now as it once was.

The Late-Life Breast Cancers and Family Risk

As opposed to the very strong genetic link for early-life breast cancers, the development of postmenopausal breast cancer appears to be much more influenced by environmental factors and much less by inheritance. But even though the genetic link is hazier, first-degree family members of these late-life breast cancer patients also suffer an increased risk for developing late-life breast cancer.

• THE DAUGHTERS AND SISTERS OF LATE-LIFE BREAST CANCER PATIENTS ARE APPROXIMATELY TWICE AS LIKELY TO DEVELOP THE DISEASE.

This degree of risk certainly represents an increase over the general population, but it's not as dramatic as the fifty times increase we just described for certain family members of premenopausal cancer patients.

Women at risk for postmenopausal breast cancer can substantially reduce the likelihood of developing the disease by carefully controlling environmental factors, which I will discuss in detail in chapter 3. Because of the slow-growing nature of late-life breast cancer, a postmenopausal woman can better her chances for a favorable outcome, should a cancer develop, by ensuring its early discovery. To do that, she must take the time to examine her own breasts each month and make a yearly visit to her physician for screening examinations and mammography. The clear need for regular medical screening in the postmenopausal (over fifty) age group cannot be overstated, and I will discuss its importance at length in chapters 4 and 5.

The Viral Culprit and the Gene

Medical scientists have long been on the trail of a viral cause for many cancers, including breast cancer. A viral relationship for certain cancers of the blood and lymph glands (leukemias and lymphomas) has already been proven. The classic example—Burkitt's lymphoma, which afflicts primarily young African children—occurs as a result of the Epstein-Barr virus, which also happens to cause infectious mononucleosis.

Could a virus cause breast cancer, too? To date, an absolute cause-and-effect relationship has not been proven, but research* suggests that there is some interconnection. A relationship between breast cancer in mice and a viral factor passed in their mother's milk has been shown. And viral particles similar to those found in the mice have been discovered in the breast milk of 60 percent of American women tested who have family histories of breast cancer, whereas they were present in only 5 percent of those women without such family history. Finding a viral particle in breast milk does not mean the virus causes breast cancer, but certainly the association is cause for further research into such a possibility.

Genetic Research and the Future

Advances in genetic research technology in recent years have made it much easier for scientists to identify specific genes that may play a part in causing diseases such as breast cancer. For instance, researchers have discovered specific spots along a chromosome in breast cancer cells where genetic material has been lost (possibly through some sort of error in duplication or some

*Schwarz, S.F., ed, *Principles of Surgery*, New York: McGraw-Hill, 1979.

kind of toxic or viral damage to the chromosome).* These deleted, or omitted, genes—the researchers believe—may be responsible for *suppressing the formation of certain types of cancer*. Stated more simply, a woman (or man for that matter) whose cells have lost this gene would be at greater risk for cancer.

Congress entered the fray of genetic testing in 1989, by earmarking $62 million to finance the Human Genome Project; they have also pledged another $3 billion to continue this work over the next fifteen years. The aim of this collaboration of genetics researchers is to identify and locate each of the 50,000 to 100,000 individual human genes that comprise the human genome and to decipher the information contained therein. Perhaps with luck and diligence, this project may unlock the secrets of inherited diseases.

Once medical scientists understand how the genome works, they may be able to predict with certainty who is at risk for an illness such as breast cancer. The practical application of these discoveries, then, lies in identifying high-risk patients. For example, the genetics specialists could test family members of cancer victims by examining their chromosomes to see if they, too, have lost the suppressor gene for that cancer. Those young women at certain risk could then begin to make informed lifestyle decisions early on about what they eat, whether to smoke or drink alcohol, how closely to maintain their ideal weight, and how often to get mammograms.

*Mackay, J. et al, "Allele loss on short arm of chromosome 17 in breast cancers," *The Lancet,* December, 1988.

Interpreting Your Genogram:
What Does it Mean?

With a basic understanding of the genetic component of breast cancer now at your command, you are prepared to interpret your family genogram. But first I want to insert a note of caution right at the beginning of this section. The chief purpose of constructing your genogram is to illustrate clearly your inherited risk for developing breast cancer, not to alarm you in any way. Discovering that this, or any disease for that matter, occurs with great frequency in your family could be upsetting. For this reason, I will repeat once again that inheriting a *risk* does not mean inheriting the *disease*. Now forge ahead with me, and let's make a realistic appraisal of your situation so that, whatever your risk may be, in subsequent chapters you can learn the positive steps you can take to lessen it.

Once you have completed your family genogram, step back and take a look at its patterns and answer the following sets of questions, which are more specific than those at the opening of the chapter:

• Do you find premenopausal breast cancer in both your mother and your sister?

• Did the cancer involve one breast or both? (Again, both relatives and both breasts mean very high risk.)

• Do you find premenopausal breast cancer in any first-degree relative (mother, sister, or daughter)?

• Can you trace premenopausal breast cancer in each generation of one side of your family tree through two or more generations?

• Do any of the related cancers (ovarian, thyroid gland, colon, brain, lungs, blood, or adrenal gland) occur in every generation of one side of your family?

If you fall into any of these categories, you should consider yourself (and your daughters) at higher genetic risk for early-life breast cancers. The more yes answers you have noted, the greater the risk. In any case, you will want to pay very careful attention to the sections on environmental promoters of breast cancer, preventive screening, and proper diet and nutrition. You should make it a point to contact the American Cancer Society chapter in your area to keep yourself in step with new research and current screening recommendations. And you may even want to seek out a breast cancer or genetics specialist in your city or area who can give you some one-on-one expert guidance and evaluate you and your family.

If you do *not* find any of these patterns, your genetic risk for early-life breast cancer is probably not substantially above normal. Now answer the following questions:

• Did your own mother or either grandmother have post-menopausal breast cancer?
• Did your sister develop a late-life breast cancer?
• Do you see a late-life breast cancer in some member of one side of your family for three or more generations?

If you have answered yes to any of these questions, you may have a somewhat increased genetic risk for the development of postmenopausal breast cancer. Remember that this kind of breast cancer has strong environmental influences, and you (and your sisters and daughters) will want to pay close attention to these controllable risk factors.

Questions and Answers

Here are answers to some commonly asked questions about breast cancer risk, which you may still have after reading this chapter.

Q: I am adopted and have absolutely no idea about any of my biological family members. How can I determine my risk?

A: As far as family history goes, you cannot—unless the agency handling your adoption maintains medical family history records on biological parents. Some of them do, and the only way to know would be to ask your adoptive parents and contact the agency. If you still cannot find out any information about your natural mother and family, your best bet would be to assume you have some family risk because you cannot prove otherwise. Follow a sensible, healthy lifestyle (maintain weight, get regular exercise, and avoid exposure to the environmental risk factors described in chapter 3). Also pay careful attention to routine health maintenance (monthly breast self-exams, annual physical exams, and regular mammograms after age thirty-five).

Q: To my knowledge, there has never been a single case of breast cancer in my family. Still, I worry about getting it. Should I?

A: Unfortunately, no one is 100 percent risk free—especially in regard to postmenopausal breast cancer, which does not seem to be tied so closely with family risk. Although your family's clean bill of health for breast cancer certainly makes it less likely that you will develop the disease, you can't lose by following a lifestyle of moderation that would reduce known risk factors for breast cancer, particularly because these factors increase your risk for other diseases as well. After the age of fifty, breast cancer risk increases for all women to some degree; therefore, even those with a small or no family risk should actively guard against the disease by getting their annual mammogram and breast exam, by following a dietary plan that keeps their weight at or near ideal, and by not smoking.

Q: I know I am at increased risk for breast cancer; it runs all through my family. What can I do?

A: First, remember what I have said: A genetic predisposition does not mean certainty of disease. You cannot change your heritage, but you can change your lifestyle. Read the next chapters carefully. They will tell you what specific steps you can take to reduce your risk.

3

The Environmental Factors

Please answer the following questions before beginning this chapter.

- Do you smoke?
- How much and for how long a time?
- Have you tried to stop smoking?
- Do you regularly drink more than three alcoholic beverages a day?
- Were you an overweight teenager?
- Are you now overweight?

- Are you 40 percent or more above your "ideal" weight (see Tables 1 and 2)?
- Is your weight presently increasing or decreasing?
- Do you carry your weight around the hips or the middle?
- Do you eat a diet high in calories?
- Do you crave sweets?
- Do sugary foods make up a significant part of daily calories?
- Do you eat red meat?
- Do you eat much tuna, mackerel, salmon, or herring?
- Did you take the birth control pill in the 1960s?
- Did you take the birth control pill as a teenager?

Depending on how you have answered these questions, your family risk for breast cancer may be high. Read on carefully to see if the lifestyle you currently lead may be contributing to an increased risk for breast cancer.

The Environment and You

From the instant of our conception, the environment in which we live begins to exert its influence on us, affecting our growth and our health. Environmental forces shape the genetic raw material from our first division as newly fertilized eggs until we mature, grow old, and finally die. Sometimes these effects benefit us; sometimes, they harm us. Often the choice is ours.

While certainly the effects of some forces of nature lie clearly beyond human control, we should not envision ourselves as powerless pieces of flotsam cast adrift on nature's raging sea. Many of the environmental factors that affect our health fall fully within the scope of our control.

Take sun exposure for example. Exposing our skin to sunlight triggers the production of vitamin D which, of course, we need for good health. Exposure to that same environmental factor in the extreme burns our skin, ages it prematurely, and predisposes us to the development of skin cancers. In effect, we determine whether this environmental force will be healthy or harmful. We must, therefore, choose a degree of exposure that will capitalize our benefits and limit our risks.

For many years, research scientists have studied the role of a number of suspected environmental triggers or factors that they felt might contribute to the development of breast cancer. But many of their findings are conflictual. One study will plainly point to a causative role for an environmental promoter and the next will show no correlation whatsoever.

Part of the confusion may be a result of researchers having viewed breast cancer as a single disease, failing to distinguish between the premenopausal and postmenopausal types. Another reason may be that often several risk factors may coexist, i.e., smokers often drink alcohol, obese women often eat high-calorie diets, and so on, and this can make it difficult to isolate the effects of specific factors. In any case, this chapter will discuss each of these suspected risk factors and give you the consensus on the most up-to-date information available.

How Do You Score?

Of the many potential contributors that might increase your risk of breast cancer, I have listed below those environmental factors that have received the closest scrutiny. Medical studies seem to bear out a stronger causal role for some of them than others, and the newest findings on a few of them may surprise you. Expert opinions vary widely in regard to the causative or promoting role for smoking in particular, but because the habit is so widespread among young women, I feel a strong medical responsibility to examine its role thoroughly. Here are the Big Six:

- Smoking.
- Daily alcohol intake.
- Obesity.
- High-calorie, high-fat diet.
- Birth control pills.
- Socioeconomic status.

Let's take a look at some of the research that has been done on each of these—pro and con—and try to get some idea of what they mean to you and your risk for the development of breast cancer and, more important, what you can do to reduce that risk.

Smoking

Who's at Risk.   Two studies have shown that premenopausal women who have ever smoked daily may have twice the risk of breast cancer than nonsmokers, and current heavy smokers may increase their risk by up to four times.

The Facts.   The many studies conducted on the association of smoking and the development of breast cancer present conflicting results. Some studies—most of which considered breast cancer a single disease—appeared to show a weak association between smoking and the risk of breast cancer; many showed no correlation between the two at all.

As I mentioned earlier, one study in Stockholm in 1975 even purported to show that cigarette smoking protected women against breast cancer, a finding the authors attributed to the fact that smoking decreases circulating estrogen levels in women. Other authors have suggested that the bizarre results of that study might be a result of the fact that as more and more young women have taken up smoking, they have begun to fall victim to the many other smoking-related diseases—such as lung cancer—which may kill them before they have a chance to develop breast cancer.

There were two medical studies I found meaningful, both of which separated breast cancer into early- and late-life cancers. One study reported in the *American Journal of Epidemiology* found that smoking seemed to be a risk factor in the development of premenopausal cancers. In this study, premenopausal women who smoked developed early breast cancers at least twice as often as nonsmokers. In addition, their risk increased in proportion to the amount smoked, so that women who had smoked more than two packs per day for as long as ten years had nearly four times the risk. Oddly enough—in view of its stronger association with environmental factors—there was no clear association between smoking and increased risk for the development of late-life breast cancers.

I want to stress here that only *two* studies have shown a clear correlation between breast cancer and smoking in young women. Many studies have failed to demonstrate this result. However, young women who may have a family history of breast cancer must try to eliminate all *possible* environmental promoters for developing the disease: For them, the issue of whether or not to smoke is an especially important one. I recommend the best and safest course for these women is to consider smoking a risk factor, as it is for so many other diseases.

To Reduce Your Risk. Stop smoking! However large or small the increase in breast cancer risk, there is simply not a single good reason to smoke. And so I can tell you without reservation that—whoever you are, whatever your risk for breast cancer—you could not do a kinder thing for yourself and those who love you than to stop smoking. In chapter 8 I have listed several medical regimens that have been successfully used to help smokers quit. Take these to your family doctor if he or she has no established program to help you quit smoking—and perhaps you can join the ranks of millions of former smokers.

Alcohol Consumption

Who's at Risk.   Women of all ages, races, and socioeconomic groups who regularly consume more than three alcoholic drinks per day may increase their risk of breast cancer about 1.5 times.

The Facts.   As of 1988, various research teams had looked into the alcohol and breast cancer association. Of the fourteen studies published by these teams, ten showed a positive correlation between alcohol and breast cancer development (to varying degrees) and four showed either no association or even a somewhat protective effect from alcohol. Of those studies that supported a causal link between alcohol and breast cancer, the strongest evidence indicated an increased risk in proportion with an increased consumption of alcoholic beverages (as reported in the *American Journal of Epidemiology*). There appeared to be a critical point (greater than three drinks per day in one study and three to nine drinks a week in others) beyond which the increased risk appeared.

But the case for a causal link for alcohol is not clear-cut. For example, on a country-by-country basis, the French have the highest per capita consumption of alcohol in the world, followed by the Italians and Portuguese. Breast cancer rates in those countries are relatively low compared with the United States, the Netherlands, Denmark, the UK, and Canada. If a direct relationship between breast cancer and alcohol does exist, why the lower rates in the three countries (France, Italy, and Portugal) that have high per capita alcohol intake? One study shed some light on this seeming contradiction by breaking down alcohol consumption into its various types—wine, beer, and hard liquor. It was found that, although some increase in risk occurred for all of the three basic types of alcohol, the strongest correlation seemed to occur with beer. In France, Italy, and Portugal, wine consumption far exceeds hard liquor and beer, which is not the case in the United States, the UK, Denmark, Canada, and the Netherlands. Apart from this difference, I could find no reasonable explanation in the studies (possible genetic factors aside) to explain the lower rates.

Because of the very strong association of alcohol consumption with other known or suspected risk factors—such as smoking, high socioeconomic level, and late childbearing or nonchildbearing—a clear-cut causative role for alcohol in the development of breast cancer has been difficult to establish. Even so, after researchers adjusted the results of the studies to take these other risk factors into account, a small but statistically significant increased risk—of 1.5 times normal—remained for women who drink moderate to heavy amounts of alcohol on a daily basis.

Alcohol may in fact be an indirect cause of breast cancer, while the risk factors with which it is often associated play a more direct role. Alcohol is more clearly a factor in the development of oral cavity, throat, larynx, esophagus, liver, and rectal cancers in women. And, of course, alcohol has long been known as the principal cause of cirrhosis of the liver. Breast cancer risk aside, medical research demonstrates enough other health problems associated with the overconsumption of alcohol to warrant limiting its use to judicious amounts.

To Reduce Your Risk. Try to limit alcohol intake to fewer than three drinks in a day, and do not drink on a daily basis. Try to keep your weekly total at three or four drinks. For women who have a strong family history of breast cancers—especially those women with first degree relatives—elimination of *any* possible risk factor may be important. For women who have little familial risk and have no other major risk factors (such as obesity, late childbearing or nonchildbearing, a history of beginning menstruation early or menopause late) the rational consumption of the occasional social drink probably carries little risk.

Obesity

Who's at Risk. Women—particularly postmenopausal women—who weigh 40 percent or more above their ideal body weight develop breast cancers nearly two times more frequently than women at their ideal weight.

The Facts. Obesity has been labeled the scourge of modern society. An estimated 32 million Americans carry excess body fat to the great detriment of their health; 7 million of them can be classified as extremely obese. Simply to list the medical studies documenting the many health problems associated with obesity could fill a book. High blood pressure, heart attacks, gallbladder disease, degenerative arthritis, diabetes, stroke, and cancer all find a common denominator in obesity.

Obese women suffer higher rates of cancer of the uterus (womb), the endometrium (uterine lining), the uterine cervix, the gallbladder, and the breast. Studies report an increased risk for some of these cancers in women who are even as little as 10 to 20 percent above their ideal body weight. The risk for breast cancer in particular rises sharply in women who weigh greater than 40 percent above their ideal.

How do you know if you're overweight? Check yourself against the height and weight tables (Tables 1 and 2), prepared by the Metropolitan Life Insurance Company.

Table 1. Desired Weights of Men Aged Twenty-five and Over

Height	Small Frame	Medium Frame	Large Frame
5'2"	128–134	131–141	138–150
5'3"	130–136	133–143	140–153
5'4"	132–138	135–145	142–156
5'5"	134–140	137–148	144–160
5'6"	136–142	139–151	146–164
5'7"	138–145	142–154	149–168
5'8"	140–148	145–157	152–172
5'9"	142–151	148–160	155–176
5'10"	144–154	151–163	158–180
5'11"	146–157	154–166	161–184
6'0"	149–160	157–170	164–188
6'1"	152–164	160–174	168–192
6'2"	155–168	164–178	172–197
6'3"	158–172	167–182	176–202
6'4"	162–176	171–187	181–207

Table 2. Desired Weights of Women Aged Twenty-five and Over

Height	Small Frame	Medium Frame	Large Frame
4'10"	102–111	109–121	118–131
4'11"	103–113	111–123	120–134
5'0"	104–115	113–126	122–137
5'1"	106–118	115–129	125–140
5'2"	108–121	118–132	128–143
5'3"	111–124	121–135	131–147
5'4"	114–127	124–138	134–151
5'5"	117–130	127–141	137–155
5'6"	120–133	130–144	140–159
5'7"	123–136	133–147	143–163
5'8"	126–139	136–150	146–167
5'9"	129–142	139–153	149–170
5'10"	132–145	142–156	152–173
5'11"	135–148	145–159	155–176
6'0"	138–151	148–162	158–179

Postmenopausal obese women especially run a significantly higher risk for breast cancer for several reasons:

1. After menopause, the ovaries no longer produce estrogen, but because estrogens can also be produced in fatty tissue, women with excess fat stores continue to maintain elevated estrogen levels of a specific type in their blood. Those tissues (breast, ovary, endometrium, and cervix) that are sensitive to this type of estrogen stimulation are then exposed to greater estrogen levels than in nonobese women for a greater period of time. This overstimulation may promote cancer growth. (Estrogens taken orally do not seem to exert the same cancer-promoting effect as those produced by the body in fatty tissue.)

2. Obese women often eat diets containing both a higher number of total calories and more fat. Research in laboratory animals has shown these diets to promote growth of tumors in the breast.

3. An excessively large breast size can hamper early diagnosis. In fatty breasts, a tiny cancerous lump the size of a pebble can easily hide from even careful examination. Mammograms help in finding these small tumors as we shall see in chapter 4.

4. Body fat can act as a reservoir for carcinogens (cancer-causing chemicals). A few years back, news of mercury-contaminated tuna fish filled the media. The tuna had picked up the poisonous mercury in trace amounts in smaller fish they had eaten. But over time, as they continued to feed on the contaminated food source, the metal concentrated more and more heavily in the fatty tissue of the tuna. Since then other heavy metals and other toxic chemicals reputed to cause cancer have turned up in the fat of cold-water fish (such as tuna, herring, and salmon). Human fat is no different; trace amounts of cancer-

causing chemicals build up in fatty tissue. The more excess fat available, the bigger the storehouse for carcinogens that could promote breast cancer.

Not only do obese women suffer breast cancer with greater frequency, they are more likely to develop it at a younger age than their normal-weight counterparts. Their prognosis for survival time after surgery if they *do* develop the disease is also substantially shorter than nonobese cancer patients.

Most of the medical studies conducted have focused on obesity in the postmenopausal age group, because of the significant risk that being overweight poses for these women. However, in view of a recently published Swedish research on high-dose birth control pills in teenagers—which suggests a striking increase in premenopausal breast cancer from stimulation by high levels of estrogens taken at an early age—overweight adolescent and teenage girls may also be increasing their risk for breast cancer through the same mechanism at work in the obese older woman: higher estrogen levels from excess conversion of estrogen precursors in fatty tissues.

To date, I do not know of a study that has tried to correlate being overweight among adolescent girls with later development of breast cancer; that topic certainly should be explored through research. However, it bears noting that overweight girls very often become overweight women, whom we already know to be at risk. Perhaps the first tiny seeds for these later-life cancers—microcancers if you will—begin their development in the earliest stages of a woman's reproductive life. If so, attaining and maintaining ideal weight through dietary intervention in adolescent and teenage girls becomes of even greater importance.

To Reduce Your Risk.   With the help and guidance of a physician, all overweight women—especially those approaching

menopause—should attempt to reduce excess body fat and tr
to reach and maintain their ideal body weight through diet ane
exercise. Overweight adolescent and teenage girls should begir
now to control their weight and strive to keep their weight a
or near their ideal throughout their lives. See chapter 8 for a lis
of books on weight loss.

Nutritional Promoters and Preventers

Let's now examine how your diet may contribute to increasing
your risk or, in other cases, offer you some beneficial preventive
protection from breast cancer.

High-Calorie, High-Fat Diet

Who's at Risk. Postmenopausal women *may* (conflicting
data) increase their risk of breast cancer by two to three times
if they consume diets high in fat and calories. There does no
seem to be a clear association for premenopausal breast cancers.

The Facts.   You've heard it before: You are what you eat. I
think we can all agree that good health depends in large measure
on proper nutrition. But what is proper nutrition? And more
important, with relation to breast cancer, what nutritional factors have an impact on your risk?

Fats.   Dietary fat intake has received a great deal of attention
from cancer researchers over the last forty years. Animal studies
(primarily in mice and rats) have consistently shown that a diet
high in fat promotes growth of mammary gland (breast) tumors
in laboratory animals. This effect led scientists to search for a
similar mechanism in human breast cancers, but because human

subjects live freely and feed at will, these kinds of studies cannot be as easily controlled. Information about daily dietary intake depends on the recall of the patients in the study, which may not always be accurate. The role of dietary fat intake in the development of human breast cancer is the subject of considerable disagreement in the scientific community, with dozens of studies supporting both sides. Because the animal studies have also shown that diets higher in total calories—with fat content remaining the same—promote breast tumor growth as well, the clear implication is that fat per se is not at fault.

So is it the calories or the fat content? And if it *is* the fat content, does the risk hold true for all kinds of fat—animal, vegetable, saturated, unsaturated, and monounsaturated? Let's take a look at some of this information and see if we can come to some sort of meaningful conclusion on this fat and calorie issue in regard to reducing your odds for developing breast cancer.

In general, breast cancer occurs much more commonly in affluent and industrialized modern cultures than in poorer, Third World countries. The glaring exception to this rule is Japan—where women have a four times *lower* risk for developing breast cancer than women in America. In part, ethnic differences may be responsible, as some research has shown that Oriental women metabolize estrogens differently than Caucasian or black women, and consequently have lower levels of certain estrogen compounds free in the bloodstream. Perhaps the lower estrogen levels makes these women less likely to develop breast cancers.

But what about dietary factors, such as fat and calories? The standard diet in Japan contains much less fat than that of Western countries, and that fact—taken together with the much lower breast cancer rates—makes the case against fat seem reasonable. Japanese women who move to Western countries and adopt Westernized (higher fat) eating habits begin to develop breast cancer at higher rates than women who remain in Japan. However, there are other factors that need to be considered before implicating fat as the culprit.

The Protective Effect of Certain Fats.   Japanese women eat greater quantities of cold-water fish than do Western women, and some evidence suggests that the fish oils (omega-3 fatty acids found in the fat of these fish) exert a protective effect against breast cancer development. The Greenland Eskimos—who traditionally ate a diet quite high in fat, but containing high levels of these omega-3 compounds—very rarely suffered from breast cancer. Perhaps it is the presence of this kind of fat, not the overall lower fat intake, that protects Japanese women from breast cancer.

It might be a good idea to add fish to your diet. Research may soon show that their omega oils help reduce risk of breast cancer, but these oils have already proven to have many other health benefits. A little later in this chapter, I have outlined some specific nutritional recommendations—including adding essential fats— that I think can help to improve your overall health as well as reduce your breast cancer risk. And I have also listed in chapter 8 where you can find such supplemental fish oil products, as well as the names of some books you might find interesting for additional reading on the subject. As always, you should check with your physician before supplementing your diet.

Is the Case Against Saturated Fats Valid?   Many authorities have attempted to implicate saturated fat and cholesterol as promoters for breast cancer; they have pointed to the higher intake of animal fat and protein in the West where breast cancer rates are higher. However, two recent, well-designed Harvard studies have shown absolutely no correlation (in either premenopausal or postmenopausal women) between cholesterol or animal protein and breast cancer, and they even seemed to show a slight protective effect from selenium (a mineral) found in red meat.

This group of medical scientists also observed that in America—because of our national obsession with lowering cholesterol by reducing saturated fat intake—we have witnessed a gradual shift away from saturated fats (butter and red meat) and eggs in favor of polyunsaturated margarines and oils. With that shift, one would expect to see a reduction in breast cancer rates, and yet the rates continue to climb. This could mean that total fat, and not just saturated fat, intake is responsible for the higher rates. But the Harvard studies did not show this to be the case. These researchers did not find any difference between breast cancer rates for diets containing 25 to 30 percent fat and those containing over 40 percent fat. They concluded that modest reductions in dietary fat would be unlikely to make any real difference in preventing breast cancer. They claimed it would take severe restriction of fat intake to levels of less than 20 percent of calories consumed to alter risk of breast cancer. Most Americans would find a diet this low in fat not only unpalatable, but unrealistic.

Conversely, another recent and widely publicized study done in northern Italy has strongly implicated dairy fat sources—milk, high-fat cheese, and butter—in causing a double or even triple increased risk in postmenopausal breast cancers among the 750 women in the group. This study showed only a very weak correlation for increased intake of meats in promoting breast cancer, but quite a strong correlation for high-fat cheeses. Other studies have failed to show the correlation between dairy fat and breast cancer. Women in Finland, for example, eat a diet rich in dairy products, yet develop breast cancer much less often than women in most Western nations.

Compared with the Finns, the women of Great Britain consume about the same percentage of their calories as fat (both roughly 40 percent), and yet the women in Great Britain suffer breast cancer at nearly twice the rate as women in Finland. Irish women, who consume about 36 percent of their calories as fat, develop breast cancer at twice the rate of Greek women, who consume the same amount of fat.

Why So Much Confusion over the Fat Issue? What factors exist to explain these differences country to country? Part of the answer—as always—may lie in inherited, ethnic (genetic) differences among the populations of the various countries—such as a different estrogen metabolism among the Japanese women. And part of the answer may lie in the known protective effect of other dietary nutrients: the omega-3 fats in cold-water fish in the diets of Japanese and Eskimos and Finns, the selenium found in red meats, and the monounsaturated oils (olive and canola oils) prominent in the Mediterranean (Greece, Italy, Spain, and Portugal). So what nutritional course should a prudent woman—particularly one already at increased risk because of other factors—follow to reduce her risk? You'll see at the end of this chapter, but for now, read on and discover the effect of too many calories and learn about all the other nutrients that could be promoters or protectors.

Total Caloric Intake

Could Total Calories—and Not Fat Alone—Be the Culprit?
The Harvard research team put forth another intriguing theory. They noted that in searching for correlations to breast cancer risk, a strong association (as some reports claim for fat intake) could be claimed for average height. Japanese women and those in underdeveloped nations tend to be short, while women of developed Western cultures tend to be taller. And women of taller stature develop breast cancer more frequently. One pos-

sible explanation for this strange association would be that in developed, affluent countries where food is abundant and calorie intake in the young is unrestricted, children grow taller. Unrestricted calorie intake in growing young women might also stimulate breast cancer genes or promoters at a critical time in reproductive development. This theory implies that the earliest stages of development of cancers might begin in adolescence.

An interesting animal study first done in 1975 and then repeated in 1986 and 1987 has shown a marked inhibition in mammary gland tumors in rats who were kept on a restricted calorie diet—even if that diet was high in fat! Most of these studies reduced daily calories to 75 percent of normal intake. A wealth of other studies have supported the finding that caloric restriction plays a beneficial role in cancer inhibition.

Sugar

Sweet as it is, numbers of medical studies have correlated the consumption of sugar with the incidence of and mortality from cancers of the breast (and the ovary, colon, rectum, and uterus). By sugar, in this instance, I mean table sugar or sucrose, although the other concentrated sources of simple sugars such as corn syrup may certainly exhibit the same effect.

As a nation, we have seen the per capita intake of table sugar alone increase from about 2 pounds per year at the turn of the century to a staggering 127 pounds—that's *per person each year*—in the United States. And right along with it, breast cancer rates continue to rise.

You may say, "But I don't use much table sugar at all! How could I possibly eat 127 pounds of sugar in a year?" Well, of course, that figure is an average of the total population. But even though you may not add table sugar by the spoonful to coffee or tea or breakfast cereal, there is enough sugar and corn syrup added to processed foods to give you quite a dose, if you're not careful. Read the label on virtually any processed food you pick up; the odds are good that it will contain either sugar or corn syrup.

Sugar, aside from being sweet, has many other qualities that make it attractive to the food-processing industry. Although I would like to think otherwise, one of sugar's chief attributes is its addictive potential. The more of it you eat, the more of it you want.

Eliminating every source of refined sugar from an American's diet would be a daunting assignment. And even trying to remove an excess of sugar from your life takes some effort—but it's not impossible. Those of you at higher risk for breast cancer, as well as your children, should aim at cutting back on sugar as a part of your overall lifestyle plan to reduce breast cancer risk.

The names of several cookbooks you might check into to help you eat a reduced-sugar diet while not feeling deprived are listed in chapter 8. Just to get you started, here are some simple rules to follow to reduce sugar intake:

1. *Avoid sugary desserts and snack foods.* Look for alternatives such as sugar-free puddings and gelatins, sugar-free popsicles, or you can now even get sugar-free and low-fat varieties of ice cream or frozen yogurt. Beware of prepackaged dessert items marked "lite" or even "diet," because these may be reduced calorie, low-sodium, or low cholesterol but still contain a load of sugar or corn syrup (or the natural alternatives of raw sugar, honey, or molasses, which in reality amount to nothing more than 80 to 90 percent plain old sugar!). You must learn to be a label reader; always check out the nutritional information on the side of the package—it will tell you total carbohydrate content in grams and often how much of that total comes from table sugar (sucrose) or other simple sugars.

2. *Switch from "regular" soft drinks to sugar-free beverages.* Sugar-free drink mixes or sodas, flavored mineral water, unsweetened tea or coffee, or just plain old water are good choices. Although they contain complex sugars, natural fruit juice is another good beverage choice.

3. *As much as possible, prepare fresh meats, vegetables, and other foods.* Only then can you be sure no sugar has been added. Again, if lack of time necessitates using prepackaged foods—as it often does for most of us—read the label and choose those with the least sugar content.

4. *Never add table sugar to sweeten when artificial sweeteners will work.* With the availability of Equal, Sweet-n-Low, Sugar Twin, and the like, and now the new product, Sweet One, which you can bake with, your need for sugar should lessen.

Fiber

While most research emphasizes fiber as an effective combatant against cancers of the intestinal tract, such as the colon and rectum, some studies—particularly one done in Israel in 1986—have suggested that a diet high in soluble fiber may also lower breast cancer risk. The mechanism by which this occurs has yet to be definitely described.

The possible protective effects against breast cancer notwithstanding, you can derive many positive health benefits ranging from bowel regularity to possibly lowering cholesterol by eating a diet higher in soluble fiber.

Most nutritional experts recommend a daily fiber intake of twenty-five or thirty grams a day at a minimum. Other sources may recommend as much as fifty grams a day, and with the national average consumption weighing in at a puny ten and fifteen grams a day, that leaves most of us way behind.

While I would agree that thirty to fifty grams of soluble fiber a day might be grand advice, if you, like most Americans, now eat a diet in the under twenty gram range, suddenly adding that much soluble fiber to your daily diet will leave you bloated, cramping, and miserable. By all means, try to increase your daily soluble fiber intake, but please, do it slowly.

I have referred to soluble fiber throughout this section, and there may be those of you who are unaware that all fiber is not the same. Fiber comes in two types: soluble and insoluble. Insoluble fiber—primarily cellulose—does not dissolve in water, neither in a glass nor in your intestine. It passes through the intestinal tract unchanged for the most part. Aside from speeding up the rate at which waste passes through the intestine, insoluble fiber (such as miller's bran and wheat bran) doesn't do much. Soluble fiber, on the other hand, does dissolve in water to form a gelatinous glue, for example, the soluble fiber in oat bran that gives oatmeal its gooey characteristics. It is this kind of fiber, soluble fiber, that benefits our health.

Good sources of soluble fiber are oat bran, rice bran, cruciferous vegetables (green leafy ones, broccoli, cauliflower, and asparagus), legumes (field peas and beans), and the psyllium fiber found in the commercially available bulk vegetable laxatives such as Konsyl, Metamucil, Citrucil, etc.

Vitamins and Minerals

No discussion of nutrition would be complete without some mention of vitamins and minerals. Most of us grew up being reminded to take our vitamins. I know my mother greeted me every morning of my life as a youngster with a cup of hot tea, some toast, and a One-A-Day Vitamin Plus Iron. She was certain (and probably not without some justification) that once out of her sight, I reverted to the burgers, fries, and sodas teenagers subsisted on then—and now. And like any concerned parent, she tried to give me the best possible nutrition at home.

In regard to breast cancer prevention, there are indeed several of these trace elements and micronutrients that may be important in your diet. And getting them in your food is safer and more effective than taking pills, so take them in pill form only as they were intended—as a supplement to a healthy diet. I have listed the U.S. Recommended Daily Allowances for these and other nutrients in chapter 8.

Folic acid. A vitamin that, as early as 1945, was reported to inhibit the growth of breast cancers. Recent work (1985 by R.L. Prentice et al, National Cancer Institute Monograph) appears to substantiate this inhibitory effect. Food sources include liver, dark green leafy vegetables, peanuts, dried beans, and whole grains.

Vitamin A. Studies suggest that certain substances present in foods containing vitamin A prevent, suppress, or retard the growth of several cancers in animals, including those of the mammary gland. Vitamin A occurs naturally only in foods of animal origin, such as liver, butter, whole milk, and egg yolks.

Beta-carotene. Beta-carotene is converted by the body to vitamin A and a 1988 Australian study has shown that beta-carotene can help prevent breast cancer. This substance has recently received a lot of play in the news media for its protective effect against lung cancer and other cancers as well. Major dietary sources, once again, are dark green leafy vegetables and yellow and orange vegetables.

Vitamin E. A large study done in England in 1986 indicated a higher incidence of breast cancer in women with low levels of vitamin E. The increased occurrence was strongest in women who also had low levels of selenium (from red meat). One theory put forth to explain these findings suggested that the two deficiencies worked together to account for the breast cancer risk increase. Dietary sources of vitamin E are vegetable oils, nuts, seeds, whole grains, and wheat germ.

Vitamin B$_6$ (Pyridoxine).   Several studies have shown a link between decreased levels of breakdown products of vitamin B$_6$ in the urine and a higher *recurrence* rate for breast cancers. Some authors suggest that vitamin B$_6$ might assist in preventing some cancers. Virtually all kinds of food contain this vitamin: meat, poultry, and fish, as well as cereal grains, fruits (especially bananas), and vegetables. So you should have no trouble getting a sufficient quantity of it from the foods you will already be trying to eat more of. And because there are some potential nerve problems associated with taking too much of this vitamin in pill form, I would caution you not to go overboard by taking it in amounts that exceed the U.S. Recommended Daily Allowance (see chapter 8).

Riboflavin (a B Vitamin).   Deficiencies in riboflavin appear to increase susceptibility to the carcinogenic effects of other cancer-causing substances. We could logically assume, based on this information, that it would better your odds against cancer not to be deficient in riboflavin. However, I could find no studies that *proved* deficiency of riboflavin affected the onset of breast cancer specifically. But because our goal here is to recommend a diet and lifestyle that will give you the best preventive advantage, I recommend you not neglect those foods that will ensure you get your quota of riboflavin. The richest food sources of riboflavin include liver, milk, and the green leafy vegetables I have already recommended to you for the other nutrients they contain.

Iodine.   A study in 1976 suggested that breast cancer rates appear to be higher in areas—such as Hawaii and Iceland—where dietary intake of iodine is high. Nutritional authorities have not deemed these results conclusive. Certainly, we need sufficient iodine in our diets to prevent thyroid problems, but it may be that too much of it can promote breast cancer. Thyroid enlargement or goiter used to be common in the parts of the United States that are far away from the oceans and where the soil (and, therefore, the foods grown in it) contained little iodine. To solve this problem, food manufacturers have for many years supplemented table salt with iodine to ensure that deficiency will not occur.

Nowadays, food grown in California, Florida, or Texas reaches people all over the country daily. That fact, coupled with the widespread availability of fresh and frozen seafood (which also contains iodine) makes it possible even for those people living inland to get enough iodine. Perhaps routinely supplementing table salt with iodine is no longer necessary.

At any rate, you can occasionally purchase noniodized salt at the grocery store, or more prudently for other health reasons, try to break the habit of using excess salt of any kind.

To Reduce Your Risk.

- Women—especially those at or near menopause—should reduce total calories consumed (to a level that will maintain ideal weight). Some sources will say to reduce by at least 25 percent of your current daily calorie intake if you're not at your ideal weight.
- Begin to use olive or canola oils in place of other animal and vegetable oils in cooking when possible.
- Be certain to eat adequate protein (at least seventy grams a day) in the form of lean red meat; cold-water fish; fowl; eggs; low-fat dairy products; and legumes such as lentils, soybeans, and peas.
- Because of the protective effect of omega-3 fish oils, supplementing the diet with high-quality omega-3 oils may also reduce risk.

- Although most authorities recommend reducing total fat intake to under 30 percent of calories, the new Harvard study casts doubt that such a reduction would reduce risk to any degree. Nevertheless, a fat reduction to this degree has been the prevailing medical wisdom. It remains to be seen if it will remain so into the next decade.
- Make sure your diet contains the recommended daily allowances of folic acid, vitamin A, beta-carotene, riboflavin, and avoid an overabundance of iodine.
- Try to slowly increase the soluble fiber in your diet to a total daily intake of at least thirty to forty grams (although no more than 100–150 grams).
- Begin now to eliminate refined sugars from your daily diet. Young girls with strong family histories of breast cancer would be well advised to follow these dietary recommendations unless their physicians advise otherwise.

Birth Control Pills and Estrogen Replacements

Who's at Risk.   Probably no one on today's drugs. There is possibly an increase of as much as five times the risk for women now in their forties who began using high-dose estrogen birth control pills while in their teens.

The Facts.   Let me begin by stating that all the new evidence seems to support no increased risk to women who take the lower dose birth control pills in use today. A recently published study (begun in Sweden in the 1960s) has shown that a group of Swedish women who began to use the birth control pill as teenagers (the high estrogen dose pills that were prescribed in the 1960s) are now developing premenopausal breast cancers at five times the expected rate. Swedish women who had already given birth or had reached the age of twenty-five before beginning these pills did not show this increase, however. These findings have led researchers to suspect that estrogen stimulation early in a woman's reproductive life may play a key role in her later developing breast cancer. Avoiding such stimulation would be of particular importance for those young women who have a strong family history for early-life breast cancer.

On the other hand, in women past menopause (whether naturally occurring or because of surgical hysterectomy) the use of estrogen replacement drugs (Premarin, Ogen, Estrovis, etc.) has not seemed to cause the increased rate of breast cancer development that research scientists once feared. If anything, in these groups of women, estrogen use offers some protection, not only against osteoporosis (bone thinning) for which physicians have long recommended that their patients take calcium and estrogens, but against breast cancer as well.

In contrast, medical evidence strongly suggests that endogenous estrogens (those made in the body) contribute to development of breast cancer. Obese women, as I explained earlier, and those women who began to menstruate before age twelve or continue to menstruate beyond age fifty-five develop breast cancers at a higher rate. Research has implicated their own naturally produced estrogens as a possible cause. Early menopause—again, whether natural or because of total hysterectomy—gives women some protection from breast cancer. The enormous gestational and prenatal spikes of hormones other than estrogen that are associated with childbirth also seem to offer some protection against breast cancer (if the birth occurs before the mother is thirty).

To Reduce Your Risk.

- Taking today's lower dose estrogen replacements at menopause may actually reduce the risk of breast cancer.

- Birth control pills now in use apparently cause no increased risk.
- Those young women with strong first-degree family histories for premenopausal breast cancers might wish to opt for another form of birth control until after childbirth or age twenty-five.
- Women who took high-dose birth control pills as teenagers (before 1970) should have annual physical exams and possibly mammograms (although their increased risk is controversial).

Socioeconomic Status

Who's at Risk. College-educated, career-oriented women with high family incomes develop breast cancer more frequently (but appear to have better survival rates) than women in lower socioeconomic groups.

The Facts. Breast cancer in the twentieth century—like gout in the seventeenth and eighteenth centuries—is a disease of affluence. Societies (or groups within a society) that enjoy unlimited access to food and drink suffer such diseases with greater regularity than impoverished ones.

Several studies have shown a strong correlation between college education, high family income, and development of breast cancer. Why should this be so? Why should better-educated people fall victim to cancers? What factor related to college attendance could possibly lead to its more frequent occurrence? Nothing. At least nothing about college itself.

Several mechanisms may be at work here to explain this phenomenon:

1. The more educated a woman, the more aware she will likely be of the danger signs of disease and the importance of regular health maintenance screening exams. Heightened awareness may bring a greater number of college-educated women to diagnosis and treatment, where their numbers add to the statistics.

2. College-educated, career-oriented women also may be more likely to postpone childbearing until later in life or elect not to have children at all, both of which research has shown to be associated with a greater breast cancer risk.

3. College-educated, career-oriented women may be more likely to consume alcoholic beverages in the course of business and social obligations, which may also increase their risk of breast cancer. (Several studies show that the use of alcohol increases directly with each year of college attended.)

4. Among female college students, a greater proportion are Caucasian than black or Hispanic. Because breast cancer occurs more commonly in Caucasian women, there would naturally be a greater percentage of these college students genetically predisposed to develop breast cancer.

5. Finally, a word about stress. Certainly, the rigors of college academic competition, intense study, loss of sleep, notoriously poor eating habits, and excessive alcohol consumption associated with college life contribute to both physical and emotional stress on students (male and female alike). How great an impact the stresses of college—and the career-oriented life that usually follows it—have on the immune system and the subsequent development of illnesses such as cancer is so far unknown. And research has shown people in unskilled work also experience high levels of stress. Because of the current crisis that medical researchers face with the AIDS virus, such topics as the impact of stress on the immune system are now receiving greater attention, and answers to these questions may soon be found.

To Reduce Your Risk.   Become informed of the known risk factors, know your own family risk, and act on this knowledge to control as many factors as possible. Get regular screening.

A Word About Breast Implants and Cancer Risk

Although having breast implants is not one of the Big Six risk factors for developing breast cancer, some concern has surfaced in the last few years about implant material used in breast augmentation mammoplasty operations (to increase the size of the breasts) possibly causing cancer. This fear arose because a certain strain of tumor-prone mice developed mammary gland cancers when exposed to the silicon gel that fills the implants. Because the kind of tumor that developed has never been seen in humans, most medical researchers did not believe these results were valid in regard to the human breast. No cases of breast cancer attributed to implants have ever been reported.

However, the implants may slightly hamper early diagnosis of breast cancers that develop due to other causes. After implant surgery, the bulk of the implant may cause the patient and her physician slightly greater difficulty in detecting small lumps on routine breast examinations, and the radiologist may have to adjust his technique to account for the implant during her mammograms. An experienced radiologist can accommodate to the implant, even though interpretation of the X ray is more difficult. None of these small obstacles should dissuade a woman from continuing a prudent course of routine breast examination.

The consensus regarding breast augmentation and cancer seems to be that implants do not place women at increased risk.

Questions and Answers

Here are answers to some commonly asked questions about environmental risk factors.

Q: My teenage daughter refuses to eat meat in any form. Like most teenagers, she fills up on french fries and soft drinks. She is not overweight, but both her father and I must watch our weight carefully. I already worry that her poor eating habits and our family tendency for being overweight might put her at higher risk for obesity, but what about for breast cancer in the future?

A: Certainly her diet is important, but its role alone in breast cancer risk later in her life is not as clear as we might like it to be. The junk-food obsession, which has our nation's teenagers (and many adults) in its grip, is a problem that worries many parents today. As far as diet itself actually increasing the risk of breast cancer, let me just say that no studies that I know of have yet been conducted to give us any hard evidence that directly implicates a high "empty-calorie" diet in teen years as causing breast cancer—except that diets high in sugar seem to promote breast cancer. However, the kind of diet your teenager eats will most assuredly increase her risk for adult obesity, and that in and of itself becomes a risk for breast cancer.

We know that excess body fat (which can occur without her appearing to be overly fat) will pose a risk for breast cancer later in her life, but the jury is still out on excess fat in the teen years. I can say, however, that in light of the wealth of laboratory information pointing in that direction, and the newly released information about estrogen stimulation in early years raising breast cancer rates in Sweden, the connection of teenage obesity and breast cancer risk may certainly be a valid one.

Those young women who *do* have a strong family risk for breast cancer should definitely begin early in life to learn the proper dietary habits that may lessen risk. Young women who come from families without such a strong family risk for breast cancer would still be well advised—for the many other health benefits proper diet can produce and the lessened chances of obesity later in life—to pay closer attention to what they build their bodies out of.

Q: My wife pays very close attention to her health and has over the last few years become a runner. She seems very fit. But she has recently begun to have problems with her menstrual periods, and this worries me, because her doctor says the running has made her female hormones low. Because female hormones and breast cancer go together, could her heavy physical activity increase her risk of breast cancer?

A: Actually, women athletes seem to have fewer cases of breast cancer than their more sedentary sisters, and most likely this is a result of low hormone levels. Heavy physical activity, such as running, biking, swimming, or even overdoing aerobic dancing can cause the levels of female hormone to drop to the point where normal menstrual cycling and ovulation do not occur. The chronically low levels of endogenous estrogen hormone, however, seem to exert a protective effect against breast cancer. This reduced risk may occur in part from a lower amount of hormones released by the ovary, and in part from the lower body fat percentage that runners—especially marathoners—commonly carry.

Q: For years I have tried to avoid caffeine to prevent cystic breast problems. Does too much caffeine promote breast cancer as well?

A: Probably not. Caffeine, which is found in coffee, tea, soft
     drinks, and chocolate, stimulates the energy-producing ma-
     chinery of the cells of the body. Many of the glandular
     functions in the body become dependent on the cascade of
     events that caffeine (and other similar chemicals in the meth-
     ylxanthine group) trigger. Scientific evidence suggested that
     excess activity in the glandular tissues of the breast driven
     by high caffeine levels might lead to fibrocystic breast dis-
     ease. On that basis, physicians advised their patients with
     cystic breast problems to avoid caffeine. Recent studies have
     not borne out the causative connection between fibrocystic
     disease and caffeine, nor have they shown any connection
     between increased caffeine intake and breast cancer.

4

Prevention

Quickly answer the following questions before reading the chapter to see where you now stand in your preventive efforts.

- Do you regularly examine your own breasts monthly?
- Do you have your breasts examined yearly by your doctor?
- If you are over thirty-five years old, have you ever had a mammogram?
- If over forty, do you have a repeat mammogram every few years?
- If over fifty, do you have a mammogram every year?
- Do you consider yourself to be upbeat and happy?

- If overweight, do you feel unable to control the problem?
- Do your family members have a positive outlook on life?
- Do your friends?
- Do you feel able to change your answers to any questions on pp. 35–36 that you saw put you at higher risk?

After answering these questions honestly, read the chapter, then come back to them and decide if you really feel you are doing all you can to prevent breast cancer.

Have you ever picked up a copy of Benjamin Franklin's *Poor Richard's Almanac*? Chances are you may have, but even if you have not, you probably grew up—as I did—being gently cautioned by its oft-quoted phrases: Early to bed and early to rise . . . , A penny saved is a penny earned, A stitch in time saves nine, and An ounce of prevention is worth a pound of cure. I find it interesting that so many of these homely truths involved prevention, advising us to take actions now to avoid problems later. While we may think of these simple phrases as old-fashioned and cliché, they have survived because they impart more than quaint wisdom. These are commonsense truths as pertinent today as they were in the eighteenth-century American colonies.

Medicine's new watchwords have become *preventive care*. Modern medical technology enables physicians to diagnose, treat, and cure more diseases now than ever before, but the real goal for the future of medical care is prevention. Stop a disease process before it begins, before it causes symptoms, before it cannot easily be controlled or cured.

For example, through the mandatory use of preventive vaccinations, smallpox has been conquered. It no longer exists as a human disease anywhere on the earth. This generation of children will not carry the vaccination scar that today's parents still do. By the same means of prevention, polio, once the rampant crippler of children, no longer poses a threat to children who receive their immunizations. No life in an iron lung awaits our sons and daughters, not because a cure has been found, but because of prevention.

Examples of prevention of infectious diseases abound in medical history—in addition to smallpox and polio, there are diphtheria, whopping cough, tetanus, cholera, influenza, measles, mumps, rubella, hemophilus, hepatitis, and some pneumonias. And through preventive care, we can conquer or control other diseases, not caused by infectious agents, as well.

Prevention Through Screening

When I was a tiny toddler, my father's mother lived at our house. She slept on a daybed in the library, because she could no longer climb the stairs to the bedrooms. My father worked a seven-day week to pay for the cost of her conventional medical treatment (which couldn't offer her much), as well as care by someone my mother referred to as "an old quack," because she doubted that his remedies would do any good. He at least gave my grandmother some kind of hope (however false) in a hopeless situation. My earliest memories involve sitting on the floor beside her bed, shaking medicine doses, and watching my mother spend hours rubbing Maw's legs to ease the pain in her bones. My grandmother was fifty-one and dying of cervical cancer, although I didn't understand it then. She died in the spring when I was almost three, and consequently, I never really got to know her.

Many women at that time—before the advent of routine Pap

smears to detect cervical cancer—suffered needlessly and died long before they should have, leaving many grandchildren who would never know them. But that story has been rewritten by routine annual preventive screening.

The routine yearly Pap smear and pelvic examination enables physicians to find cervical cancers at very early stages when they have not yet even invaded on a microscopic level and when surgical treatment can effect a cure. A woman in America today never need suffer the ravages of this disease, if she takes advantage of the widespread availability of inexpensive screening.

Finding breast cancers earlier through preventive screening methods—breast self-examination, clinical examination by a physician, and mammography—will ultimately reduce the number of needless deaths (now at over 40,000 women per year in the United States alone) from this disease, as well. The clear necessity for preventive screening of those women at higher risk for developing breast cancer cannot be overstated. Because these methods of prevention are so important to the early diagnosis of breast cancer, and because early diagnosis leads to much improved chances for cure, I have devoted most of chapter 5 to an in-depth discussion of how and when to do the breast self-examination and much of this chapter to the current recommendations regarding who should receive screening mammography and when. But let's turn first to some other important aspects of prevention.

Preventive Thinking

Now that you have read the first three chapters of this book, you should have some idea of your own family risk for breast cancer. You have learned what environmental factors contribute to increasing your risk and what you can do to reduce it. If you now know that you (or your sister, mother, or daughter) fit the breast cancer description, at any level of risk, you should begin to practice preventive thinking.

Although you should certainly recognize the implications of your heightened risk, you can become your own worst enemy if you allow yourself to have a fatalistic outlook about your chances for developing a breast cancer. Recognition of risk should only serve to make you more aware of the disease and more vigilant in controlling those risk factors that you can.

I have learned in the ten years I have been at the practice of medicine never to discount the powerful force of a patient's psyche: it either can be a strong ally or a hindrance in a person's response to treatment and recovery. The patient who *expects* to get well, will very often do so even in the face of a poor prognosis. On the other hand, the patient with a negative attitude usually responds much less favorably, has a slower recovery, and more frequent complications.

Remember, being at risk just means *being at risk*. You should be aware of your risk, but you shouldn't *expect* the worst; plan instead to stay well. Your positive attitude, coupled with positive actions—such as eliminating or reducing the known risk factors we've discussed, as well as having routine screening examinations—will make a big difference in whether risk becomes reality.

Taking Positive Action

Granted, you can't change the fact that you may have exposed yourself to certain risk factors in the past, and you can't alter your genetic makeup, but instead of bemoaning your fate, take action.

Eliminate Risk Factors from This Day Forth

• *Control your weight.* If you think you carry too much body fat, find out. A number of tables to help you calculate your body fat percentage can be found in diet books or possibly from your physician (see chapter 8). If you are overweight, begin a program to safely reduce your weight through a combination of diet and gentle daily exercise.

• *Stop smoking.* The only sure means to effectively shake a cigarette habit must come from within you. Until you truly embrace the notion that you must stop smoking, no method will help you. Once you have made the mental commitment to quit, the rest comes easily. If you smoke and want to quit, join a local stop smoking program.

Often local hospitals have outpatient stop smoking programs, or you can ask your physician to assist you with behavior modification classes and the prescription gum, Nicorette. Chapter 8 has a list of a number of successful therapeutic regimens to help you stop smoking with the help of your physician. In addition to private physicians, many outpatient clinics have sprung up across the country to assist smokers in kicking the habit. Psychologists who are experts in hypnosis may be able to help you, or you may respond to your own self-help hypnosis using subliminal cassette tapes.

If you rarely smoke and only in certain situations, such as at parties or playing cards, choose other activities. Avoid those groups of people with whom you smoke. Quit with help or quit cold turkey, but take positive action *today* to eliminate this risk factor from your life.

• *Limit your alcohol intake.* Although your business or social life may frequently place you in situations in which you may be tempted or even encouraged to imbibe freely, you must take control of the situation and set your limits. Restraint and moderation must become your watchwords. One glass of wine or champagne, one mixed drink, or one beer now and then do not appear to increase your relative risk. If you drink regularly, after that first drink, you should switch to a nonalcoholic alternative.

Surround Yourself as Much as Possible with Upbeat People

Don't let yourself become the victim of the negative attitudes of friends, family, or even your spouse. My father always used to say, "You can't lie down with a skunk without picking up some of the stink," and he was right. He used this colorful, if somewhat graphic, description when I was a teenager to illustrate the importance of choosing respectable friends. But the sentiment applies just as well to the importance of a positive attitude. If you find yourself in the constant company of negative, complaining, dissatisfied people, before very long you will find yourself adopting their sour attitude. Approaching every day from an angry or disgruntled standpoint takes its toll on your mental health and physical well-being as well. Choose, instead, to surround yourself with friends and family who take an optimistic outlook on life, who approach a difficult situation as a challenge not an obstacle. Let their positive viewpoint rub off on you. Don't let yourself be put in the role of a helpless victim. Even though you may come from a family rife with breast cancer, if you *plan* to stay well, *plan* to be a survivor, your positive attitude can do nothing but improve your chances. You must view yourself as being in command of your life and health, because in fact, you are.

Remove Yourself from Situations That Lead You Astray

If you eat more when you're in front of the television, either strike a bargain with yourself that you forbid food consumption except at the table, or turn off the tube and read a good book, or take a walk instead. Protect your diet plan from sabotage in your weaker moments by not filling the cupboards with boxes of junk food that you'll be tempted to eat. Defend yourself against your own weaknesses.

Don't make the snacking habits of children, spouses, or others who live with you be your excuse for keeping chips, cookies, pies, and cakes at hand. If the rest of the family can't or won't see the wisdom of healthy eating habits, let them feed their addictions elsewhere.

If ducking into the local fast-food palace wreaks havoc with your diet, don't duck in. You're in control. No one else. You alone are responsible for your life and health. If you truly want to reduce your risk, you must recognize your weaknesses and protect yourself from falling victim to them. When you find yourself tempted to stray, take just ten seconds to examine the risk versus the benefit. In each instance, ask yourself this question: Which of us is stronger, me or this chocolate fudge brownie delight . . . or this cigarette . . . or my desire to lie abed instead of getting up for my morning walk. When you can answer "*I am,*" then you've made a choice for health one more time. I urge you to approach all your lifestyle changes this way: one instance at a time. You won't believe the exhilaration you'll feel every time you take control of your life.

Don't Ignore the Need for Preventive Screening

Although I urge you to plan to stay well, if you are at high risk, you must face your fears about breast cancer, recognize it as a danger, and take steps to ensure your survival. If you have been putting off making an appointment for your annual breast examination with your doctor, or for your mammogram, or your Pap smear and pelvic examination, write yourself a note now to make that appointment. And keep the appointment. Your peace of mind and continued good health are worth the effort.

To effectively protect yourself, you must know when and how to screen yourself, what to look for, and what to expect in physician examinations and mammography. In the next sections, I will introduce you to self-examination of your breasts and take you through the mammographic exam. I hope that knowing what to expect will allay any apprehension you may feel about confronting your risk head on.

And then, later, for those of you who may now have friends or relatives facing treatment for breast cancer, I will discuss other currently used diagnostic tests and the available treatments. I do not want any of you to assume that the sections on diagnosis and treatment mean that developing a breast cancer is the inevitable outcome for those at risk—*it is not!* My intent here is not to worry you; I simply felt that there may be readers among you who will want—or need—to have this information.

The Best Defense Is a Good Offense: Early Diagnosis Through Self-Examination

Breast self-examination remains the cornerstone of early diagnosis of tumors. Women discover most cancers—in fact as many as nine out of ten—themselves, and for this reason, every woman should learn how and when in her monthly cycle to perform a complete breast exam. Most local chapters of the American Cancer Society have ongoing programs to teach women breast examination techniques and will be happy to help you if you think you may not be performing the examination properly. In addition, the American Cancer Society and the National Cancer Institute have some helpful how-to brochures that they will send to you at no cost. I have listed these sources of information and others in chapter 8.

If you already know how to examine your breasts and when, a short review course can't hurt, but for those of you who have never attempted self-examination and may not know how to go about it, I have devoted a good portion of chapter 5 to showing you how to examine your own breasts in a step-by-step fashion.

Prevention Through Early Detection: The Mammogram

Properly performed, physical examination of the breast can detect lumps as small as 0.5 to 1.0 inch in size. Detection of earlier, smaller tumors that cannot be felt even by the most expert examiner can be made by mammography, in some cases as much as one to two years sooner. In cancers found in their earliest stages, before even microscopic invasion has taken place, cure rates approach 100 percent. Prognosis for cancers that have already widely spread to distant sites is much poorer, with only 10 percent of such women still surviving after five years.

For those of you who have never had a mammogram, let me begin here and acquaint you with this powerful ally in your preventive life plan.

What Is a Mammogram?
The mammogram is nothing more than a special kind of X ray that uses very low levels of radiation to look through the breast. During the examination, the breast is flattened and held in place between two radiographic plates while the mammo-

graphic technician takes an X-ray picture of the breasts in various views. The actual process is really not very different from taking an X ray of a foot, arm, or your teeth.

Recent advances in mammographic technology and better equipment allow doses of well under one rad (a very small amount of radiation) for a full examination including four views of the breasts. Early mammography equipment that exposed women to higher radiation levels caused some concern among health care professionals and laypeople alike who feared that frequent screening might actually promote cancer development in the breasts. Certainly, had the older style mammography machines remained in use, physicians and their patients would have had greater cause for such concern. However, since the advent of the newer, better equipment that we use today, the fear of an increased risk from radiation during the exam should no longer deter women from participating in routine screening by mammography. You might wish to ask your physician, or the mammographer, to be certain that the total dose of radiation used during your examination will not exceed one rad. There is no need to expose yourself to a higher dose on a yearly screening exam.

How Does a Mammogram Show Cancer?
Small doses of X ray can easily penetrate fatty tissue in the older breast, but are absorbed by denser tissues in younger breasts. Because the breast after age thirty-five contains a progressively greater amount of fat and less glandular and fibrous tissue, abnormally dense areas of breast tissue (such as cancerous lumps that will not allow the X rays to pass them as well) can be easily seen. They will show up as whiter or lighter areas on the X-ray film. Cancers, in particular, display characteristic patterns of whitening on the mammogram, which enables expert

radiologists to diagnose them. Remember, more than 90 percent of breast cancers can be detected on mammogram, many of them before they can be felt on examination.

Mammography has not been routinely recommended before age thirty-five, because the denseness of the young breast makes accurate examination difficult. Mammography in this younger age group has usually been reserved for assisting in the diagnosis of a lump that can already be felt and requires a radiologist very skilled in reading mammograms to interpret the picture. But it certainly can be done.

Women in families where breast cancer (or the related cancers of the colon, thyroid, ovary, and adrenal gland) appears in every generation, should begin mammographic screening at a *very* early age—some experts suggest as early as twenty-five. And, of course, monthly breast self-examination should be the cornerstone of every woman's risk-reduction program.

Who Should Have a Mammogram?
The American Cancer Society generally recommends

- Every woman between thirty-five and forty should have her first mammogram.
- Women past forty should have a mammogram every one to two years.
- Women past fifty should have a mammogram every year.

In addition:

- High-risk women should probably have mammograms at least yearly after age twenty-five.

Because two-thirds of all breast cancers occur after the age of fifty, the general recommendation has always been that age fifty be the starting point for yearly mammography among the population as a whole. The value—measured in lives saved—in the postmenopausal age group of early detection of cancer through mammography has been unequivocally established.

In the past, studies did not demonstrate as clear and direct a lifesaving effect for screening those women between forty and fifty, and consequently some disagreement has arisen among cancer specialists regarding the benefit of routine annual mammography among women in this age group. However, a recently completed study on breast cancer deaths prevented by mammography among women in their forties *has* clearly shown a benefit. And now, some researchers feel that women in this age group benefit from yearly screening to an even greater degree than those over fifty.

The generally recommended ages for mammography apply to women of normal or slightly increased risk. Without a doubt, those women at higher risk—in particular, those who have identified a strong family risk for the directly inherited premenopausal breast cancer—warrant much closer medical follow-up. These women should have their first mammogram at twenty-five and then be followed-up with repeat screening mammograms every year. Several new studies have confirmed that because of their fast-growing nature, the breast cancers that develop in the premenopausal age group could appear and grow substantially in the time between a two- or three-year screening interval. Consequently, the value of early detection in this high-risk group warrants more frequent screening.

Is the Mammographic Examination Painful?

It seems the next greatest fear after that of exposure to radiation during the exam, is that the mammogram will hurt. Because I have now reached the age at which I should have my baseline mammogram—I am thirty-six—I decided that perhaps now would be a good time for some firsthand research. I made and kept my appointment, just as I have urged each of you to. For the record, I am not in a high-risk group—for breast cancer, at least—but, because I recommend a baseline mammogram for all my normal-risk female patients between thirty-five and forty, it seemed only fair to practice what I preach.

From my hands-on research, I quickly learned that any discomfort caused by squeezing the breast tissue between the radiographic plate and the plastic compressor plate—while certainly tight—couldn't compare with the shock of my bare skin on the cold metal plate. They really should warm those things up! However, I can attest that, while certainly not totally painless (I would describe it as mildly uncomfortable) having a mammogram caused me no greater pain than having dental X rays. Although I wouldn't classify either experience as enjoyable, I can honestly say that the prospect of my next one does not cause me the least concern in regard to pain.

Interestingly, I found a study in which Harvard researchers actually polled women regarding the degree of pain they experienced during mammography. Of the 1,847 women surveyed, 90 percent said that they felt little or no discomfort, and only 1 percent described a substantial degree of pain; even among this 1 percent, none of the women felt the degree of pain would stop them from having a mammogram in the future.

Breast size plays some role in determining the comfort level of the examination. Women who have small breasts usually find the squeezing required during the examination a bit more painful than women with larger, more pendulous breasts. And of course, women with tender, cystic breasts will experience a greater degree of discomfort as well.

What Is Xeromammography?

A xeromammogram differs little from a standard mammogram in regard to how the test is done. However, this technique has a slightly better chance of showing certain kinds of abnormal patterns, such as calcium deposits. The xeromammogram technique requires a slightly higher radiation exposure, and for this reason, as a screening technique, the standard mammogram is often preferred. On the plus side, however, xeromammograms require less flattening of the breasts, and may be a good alternative for women with extremely tender, cystic breasts who find standard mammography too uncomfortable.

A Word about the Cost of Mammography and Insurance Coverage

The cost of a standard screening mammogram will naturally vary from city to city, but generally runs in the neighborhood of $80 to $100. While this amount of money may seem prohibitive at first glance, consider that at most, this means spending about twenty-five cents a day over the course of a year for a test that could be lifesaving. That's pretty cheap insurance.

Fortunately, as more and more mammographic screening centers open to handle the increasing demand for this examination, the cost of routine mammography will begin to come down. Also, some local American Cancer Society chapters have programs that assist in subsidizing the cost of screening to some degree. With their help, the cost can drop to as little as $40.

Several states—Texas, California, Maryland, Kansas, and Massachusetts—have already passed laws to require insurance companies to cover the cost of routine mammograms for many age groups. Other states are sure to follow suit. And now, for those patients over sixty-five, mammograms may be included in Medicare coverage under the catastrophic-care bill, but that legislation has yet to make it through Congress.

The Golden Triangle of Breast Cancer Prevention

The symbol of the triangle or pyramid has since the times of the Egyptians been thought to have protective power. These three basic steps in a breast cancer preventive strategy form the triangle:

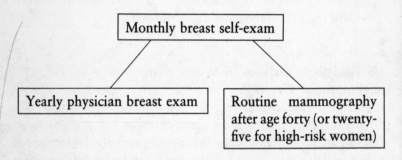

Monthly breast self-exam

Yearly physician breast exam

Routine mammography after age forty (or twenty-five for high-risk women)

The power of this triple strategy in bettering mortality statistics for breast cancer should not be underestimated. This triple-teaming approach is your best bet for ensuring early detection, and as I have repeatedly said, early detection offers the best prognosis for cure should breast cancer develop. Remember, found in its earliest stage, breast cancer is nearly 100 percent curable.

Questions and Answers

Q: I had a "breast job" done to enlarge my bust line. Afterward I had to have an operation to break up the scars that had formed. My plastic surgeon told me that my body had reacted to the implant with fibrosis. What does this really mean, and does it put me at risk for breast cancer?

A: Some women do suffer excessive scarring of the chest wall tissues around the implant after augmentation mammoplasty (cosmetic breast implants to increase size). Much like the reaction that an oyster has to a grain of sand, the silicon gel may invoke a kind of sealing-off response, with the body laying down layers and layers of dense fibrous tissue (fibrosis) to wall off the implant from the rest of the body. Occasionally, this reaction is so severe that it may necessitate removal of the implant. Laboratory studies into the cancer-causing potential of the silicon gel (which fills the implant and gives it its supple shape and feel) have failed to demonstrate an increased risk for the development of cancer in human breast tissue.

Q: I have breast implants and have never had a mammogram, because I worry that the squeezing of the machine might rupture my implants. Could this happen?

A: The compressor apparatus of the machine certainly does squeeze tightly, but not to the point that it would rupture a breast implant. Let me illustrate the resilient nature of the implants by a comparison. After augmentation mammoplasty, some women have severe fibrous scarring that deforms the shape of the implant, and their surgeons must sometimes perform what is called a closed capsulotomy, for which they strongly squeeze the breast and implant between the heels of their hands. I have seen this maneuver performed, and even attempted to perform it myself on a patient without much success. Although I am no weakling, I simply didn't have the strength to break up the scar tissue even when squeezing as hard as I possibly could. I can attest that the force surgeons exert on the breast during a closed capsulotomy is far and away harder than the squeezing produced by the mammography machine, and they rarely rupture an implant. Have your mammogram, and don't fear.

Q: My mother (who is past menopause) had a mammogram several years ago. It was normal, but her doctor says she needs one every year. Does she really need it repeated? This just seems like a waste of her money.

A: Yes, yes, absolutely yes, she should have it. All women past the age of fifty should have a screening mammogram every year. Having a single normal mammogram is lovely, but it just means that all is apparently well at that time. Repeating the examination every year will ensure that a cancer that might arise in the intervening year is found early. The cost is a small one in view of the benefit.

5

Identifying the Symptoms

To learn to examine your breasts correctly, you should know something about breast anatomy, so let's begin there.

The Structure of the Breast

The breast (Figure 3) consists of fatty tissue, supportive fibers, and glandular (or milk-producing) tissue. The breasts of young women contain much less fat and consequently feel much firmer. Age and childbearing cause a softening of the breast tissue both through the gradual replacement of glandular tissue with fatty tissue and the stretching of supportive fibers. But it is in the mammary (breast) gland itself that most of the action takes place. This gland consists of clusters of milk-producing cells, referred

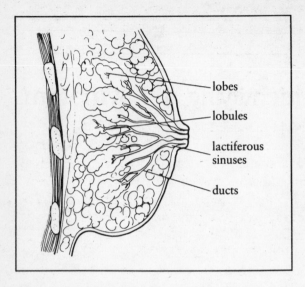

Figure 3. Breast cross section.

to as lobules, and drainage ducts. The lobules group together to form about fifteen to twenty lobes in the breast each attached to a hollow drainage tube (a duct) that travels through the breast to empty into the nipple. The nipple, itself, can develop a special kind of cancer—called Paget's disease—which we will discuss later in this chapter.

Most of the diseases that cause lumps in the breast, including cancerous ones, arise in the lobules or ducts of the glandular tissue portion of the breast. The lobes and lobules change during the monthly menstrual cycle, swelling and becoming more tender in response to drops and surges of the various female hormones. When these changes occur, you will notice that your breasts will feel fuller and more lumpy. Because most breasts have a some- what lumpy feel—especially in certain women—you will need to become familiar with the normal lumpiness of your own breasts at various times in your monthly cycle. Only then can you become aware of a persistent change in the breast tissue that should prompt a visit to your physician.

The Benefits (and Risks) of Breast Self-Examination

Who Should Examine Their Breasts?

I saw a recent survey that stated that only 25 percent of women perform a routine breast exam monthly, and, frankly, this shamefully low figure shocked me. No other routine self-test designed to detect disease early can compare in importance. As I have already stated, greater than 90 percent of breast cancers are found initially by the woman herself, not by her physician.

I cannot overstate the importance of monthly breast self-examination for every woman over thirty years of age, and after age twenty for very high risk women. To underscore how important I view this advice to be, let me state it again:

- EVERY WOMAN PAST THE AGE OF THIRTY SHOULD BECOME PROFICIENT IN PERFORMING THE MONTHLY BREAST CHECK AND SHOULD DO SO MONTH IN AND MONTH OUT FOR THE REST OF HER LIFE.

Why thirty? Why not sooner? The American Cancer Society still recommends that all women over the age of twenty examine their breasts monthly. However, a medical study done recently in Toronto, Canada, has shed some new light on this seemingly harmless practice. Because cancer of the breast—except in those 9 percent of cases where there is direct inheritance of a gene— occurs so rarely before the age of twenty-five or thirty and because benign breast lumps (such as fibrocysts and fibroadeno-mas, which I'll describe shortly) occur very often in the late teens and twenties, advising all young women to check their breasts monthly has at least some potential for harm. Many believe the benefits simply don't justify the trauma for *normal-risk* women under the age of thirty. Let me explain why.

Evaluation of a Benign Breast Mass

Persistent lumps detected in the young breast must be eval-uated by a physician, and because of the very high likelihood that any breast lump in a very young woman not at high risk for breast cancer will be benign (not harmful), the cost in terms of physical and emotional discomfort as well as dollars must be considered. Even in the most highly skilled hands, the true nature of a breast lump cannot be clearly identified solely by feeling the breast. From the moment the evaluation of the lump begins, at least some small measure of emotional strain begins for the patient (and her physician), some degree of worry about the discomfort of whatever procedure may be needed, or about the nature of the lump itself. Is it just a harmless knot in the breast or something more? Further testing will have to be done, perhaps involving a mammogram or one of the procedures de-scribed below.

Whether or not you are at high risk for breast cancer, you (or one of your family members) may need to undergo an evaluation for a breast lump at some point in your life. It may help allay your fears to understand why one or more of the following procedures or tests your doctor may suggest are necessary.

The following procedures help your physician to identify a breast lump.

Aspiration of a Cyst. If the lump has a cystic (fluid-filled sack) feel, the physician may elect to try to withdraw some of the fluid with a hypodermic needle—in effect to drain the cyst. Although the fluid may be sent to the pathologist to be examined under the microscope for cancerous cells, fluid-filled cysts in women under thirty do not usually demand further evaluation, because they are virtually never dangerous. But among women at high risk for cancer, even these fluid-filled cysts may demand a more thorough check.

Fine-Needle Biopsy. Solid lumps, however, present a more difficult diagnostic problem. Their evaluation will most likely require either a diagnostic mammographic examination, a needle biopsy, or open surgical biopsy. The needle biopsy, like draining the fluid, can be done in the physician's office under a local anesthetic. Instead of drawing off fluid, the physician will draw some of the cells from within the lump up into a hollow needle. If the pathologist cannot identify any cancerous cells under the microscope, that doesn't necessarily prove that the lump is not a cancer. The lump will still need to be checked repeatedly by physical examination and mammography, if possible, and may ultimately still have to be removed by open surgical biopsy.

Open Surgical (Excisional) Biopsy. In this procedure, the surgeon will open a small area of skin overlying the lump and will remove the entire lump for the pathologist to examine under the microscope. The biopsy of a very small breast lump may require only a local anesthetic (injected with a needle in a fashion similar to that used by the dentist or by your doctor to repair a cut) to ensure patient comfort; a larger lump might require the use of a general anesthetic (being put to sleep for surgery) to remove the mass from the breast comfortably.

When in the Month Should You Examine Your Breasts?

In timing the menstrual cycle, you should count the day bleeding begins as day one. By day seven, the hormonal changes that promote lumpiness of the breasts have subsided sufficiently to permit a good examination. Therefore, women who have not yet reached menopause should examine their breasts on day seven of their cycle, *seven days from the start of their menstrual period*. To better understand what happens to the lumpy character of your breasts under the influence of female hormones, you might also want to examine your breasts a few times just before your menstrual period begins and again on about day fourteen of the cycle (the hormonal surge that causes ovulation occurs about then).

Women who no longer menstruate because of natural or surgical menopause may choose any day of the month to examine their breasts. I would recommend choosing a date and making it the same one every month. As with any task, you will find it easier to remember to do your monthly breast examination if you keep the routine the same.

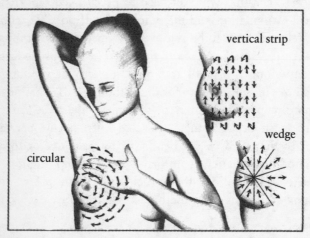

Figure 4. Breast self-examination.

How to Examine Your Breasts Step-by-Step

Standing Before a Mirror in Good Light

1. Place your hands on your hips. Do your breasts appear symmetrical (alike) in size? shape? contour? Does the skin appear normal? Are there any areas of dimpling? Any areas of skin that have an "orange peel" appearance? Any redness or scaling?

2. Raise your arms above your head. Do you notice any difference between your breasts now in shape or contour?

3. Now place your left arm behind your head and with the right hand, feel the entire breast from the armpit to the breastbone with the flat of your fingers, not the tips. Move across the breast in a pattern, so that you will cover all areas. You may choose to use a circular or clocklike motion, or examine vertical strips or wedge-shaped sections as shown in Figure 4. (Women with larger breasts may need to support the breast with their left hand instead of holding that arm behind the head.) Use a gentle but firm amount of pressure to feel for lumps with a circular, rubbing motion.

4. Now examine the right breast in the same manner.

Next, Lying Down Comfortably

1. Flatten your left breast by placing a pillow under the left shoulder blade and raising your left arm.

2. Using your right hand with the flat of the fingers, again feel the entire left breast from armpit to the center of the breastbone. Feel for lumps by making small circular, rubbing

motions with the flat of your fingers, following one of the patterns as before to cover all areas of the breast.

3. Examine your nipple and surrounding area (the areola) for scaling or redness, then *gently* squeeze the nipple between your thumb and middle finger to see if you can express any fluid. I emphasize the gently, because with too vigorous squeezing, the nipple may discharge some fluid normally.

4. Repeat the procedure for the right breast.

In the Shower or Bathtub

You may wish to use this time when your skin is wet to feel the breasts again, following the directions for the standing examination. Many of my patients tell me they find the lumps easier to feel when their skin is wet.

Checking Your Technique

Once you feel you have mastered the exam, you might wish to check your technique to be sure you have it down. At your yearly breast examination (and Pap smear), ask your doctor to watch you perform the examination. Don't be shy about asking for tips about how you can improve your method. In addition, the American Cancer Society's local chapters, as well as local hospitals often sponsor breast examination and screening programs to help educate women about proper technique. These groups will often have model breasts—complete with lumps of various sizes—for you to practice on.

Another source of information on how to perform an excellent breast exam is available through the MammaTech corporation. This exam—called MammaCare—teaches a slightly more involved method of breast palpation using a crisscross pattern and varying finger pad pressure to detect lumps at different depths.

I have listed their address and toll-free telephone number in chapter 8 should you want to find out where you can be trained in the MammaCare technique.

What if You Find a Lump in Your Breast?

If you feel a lump in your breast what should you do? What does it mean? Certainly, you should have your physician take a look at any lump you find at a quiet (hormonally inactive) time in your menstrual cycle. If you should happen to find the lump just before your period is due to begin (about days twenty to twenty-eight of the menstrual cycle) or at the midcycle ovulation hormone surge (about day fourteen), try to ignore it until your menstrual period has ended and recheck your breasts on day seven. As difficult as it may be to do so, make an effort to leave the suspected lump alone. Continuously feeling for the lump to see if it is still there will only make it more swollen and tender. If the lump persists through day seven of your cycle, see your doctor. Unless the lump feels like a cyst, don't be surprised if the doctor advises you to wait until a different point in the cycle and return for a repeat examination.

Breast Lumps:
What's the Difference Between Them?

As frightening as the discovery of a lump may be, I urge you to remember that most breast lumps prove to be benign, or harmless. This is true even for women at high risk for breast cancer. If you should ever discover a lump in your breast, do not become alarmed. You and your physician can sort out its cause together, and in most instances you will find that the lump is of no consequence.

Causes of Benign Lumps

Injury.   A bump or bruise on the fatty tissue of the breast may leave a tender knot that may persist for weeks. Often the overlying skin discolors, but sometimes no visible bruise forms. These lumps will resolve on their own with no treatment beyond warm compresses and time.

Drug Reaction.   Some medications can stimulate fullness, lumpiness, and tenderness in breast tissue; some examples are:

Blood pressure medications	Aldactone (a diuretic) Aldomet (alpha-methyldopa)
Heart medications	Digoxin and Lanoxin (digitalis) Inderal, Lopressor, Tenormin, and Visken (beta-blockers)
Antipsychotic/antinausea drugs	Compazine (chlorpromazine)
Ulcer medications	Tagamet (cimetidine)

Although drug-induced breast lumps occur in both men and women, they actually arise more frequently in men. This difference may simply be one of breast size. In the smaller, less-dynamic male breast, a little swelling and discomfort doesn't escape notice as readily. The treatment, of course, involves stopping any drug that might be causing the problem, but resolution of the lump may take several weeks. Any lump that persists beyond that time must be evaluated for other causes.

Fibrocysts. Benign lumpiness that develops from the supportive and glandular portions of the breast are fibrocysts. The cysts are small fluid-filled sacks that can swell and become tender in response to the changes in hormones that occur monthly.

Medical research into the causes of this usually harmless but painful condition at one time implicated caffeine. Physicians advised women with cystic mastitis (as the condition is also called) to cut out coffee, colas, tea, chocolate, and other foods that contained caffeine. In many cases, the painful cysts seemed to respond. Newer studies, however, have failed to substantiate a causative role for caffeine, but you may want to cut down your intake on general principle. Women with severe cases of fibrocystic change often find relief through use of the prescription drug Danocrine (a potent hormone), but physicians usually reserve this drug for disabling cases of cystic mastitis.

Fibroadenomas. These slow-growing, harmless tumors have a firm almost rubbery feel on examination. They, too, develop from the supportive and glandular structures of the breast under stimulation of estrogens, but do not develop fluid spaces. Because these tumors respond to estrogens, they may grow more rapidly during pregnancy. Their rapid growth and solid nature has traditionally forced physicians to resort to needle or open surgical biopsy to be sure of the diagnosis of these benign tumors.

A new application of a pair of older diagnostic tests—the ultrasound examination and the Doppler flow study—may make biopsy of suspected fibroadenomas less necessary. Both of these tests are safe and painless, and unlike the mammogram, they are not hampered by the denseness of the young breast. Moreover, they do not rely on X rays. In the ultrasound test—just like those used on pregnant women to "see" the baby's heartbeat—harmless sound waves pass through the breast and bounce or echo off tissues within it. A solid lump echoes with a different pattern than a fluid-filled one.

The Doppler study, on the other hand, detects the sounds emitted by the pumping of blood and thus determines the amount of blood flowing to the lump each time the heart beats. Fibroadenomas swell and become more active during certain times of the menstrual cycle and recede and become quiet at others—something a cancerous lump does not do. These predictable cycles in how blood flows to the lump indicate that it is not cancerous.

Not every breast lump will be totally innocuous. For example, some breast lumps are not cancers but are prone to become so. We term these breast changes *precancerous* lumps.

Precancerous (Premalignant) Lumps

Intraductal Papillomas.   Tumors of this type are not yet considered cancers, but because they contain some of the earliest features of cancerous change, specialists believe that they may represent cancer precursors. Because such growths arise from the cells lining the inside of the ducts leading to the nipple, a bloody discharge from the nipple usually occurs as the first symptom—even before a lump can be felt. At this early stage, your doctor may refer you for a special kind of X-ray examination called a *ductogram*. In this test, the radiologist inserts a small blunt-tipped needle into the duct opening, injects a thick contrast dye into the duct, and takes X rays as the dye fills the duct. Areas of narrowing—which might represent small growths— can then be seen. Because these growths can precede a cancerous change, surgeons usually advise that they be removed.

Fibrocysts with Atypia.   The vast majority of fibrocysts pose no increased risk for breast cancer whatsoever. Some cases fail to resolve and ultimately come to open surgical biopsy, however, and in about 4 percent of these lumps the pathologist finds *atypical epithelial hyperplasia,* which is an abundance of abnormalities in the cells that line the ducts and glands. However, these lumps are still not classified as cancerous. Specialists debate the significance of these changes, but most agree that a woman whose fibrocystic lumps have this pathologic feature may be at increased risk for developing breast cancer later and should be followed more closely by her doctor.

Although the odds that any breast lump will be benign are in your favor, one can never know. There is always the possibility that any lump *could* be cancerous—hence the need for careful evaluation.

To fight any enemy, it is important to know what it is you're fighting. And so, I want to unmask the enemy with you now, not because you will necessarily have to face breast cancer—my fervent wish is that you will not—but because to know your enemy is to gain advantage over it.

The Cancers of the Breast

Malignant tumors of the breasts are termed *carinomas* because they affect lining membranes rather than connective tissue. Pathologists and cancer specialists classify breast cancers based on several criteria:

- How the cancer looks and feels—giving rise to such complicated names as comedocarcinoma, scirrhous adenocarcinoma, colloid carcinoma, and medullary carcinoma.
- What structure the cancer arose from—such as the milk duct cells in ductal carcinoma, the duct-lining cells in in-

traductal carcinoma, or the glandular or milk-producing cells in lobular carcinoma.
- The aggressiveness of the cancer—infiltrative or noninfiltrative carcinoma (meaning whether or not the disease tends to actively invade the surrounding tissues).

For ease of discussion, let me divide the cancers of the breast according to where they arise: the ducts, the gland, and the nipple. Other elements of the breast structure—the fat, the muscle, and the fibrous support framework—can develop cancers, too, but these occur quite rarely and aside from being geographically located in the breast, should not be considered "breast cancers" for the purposes of this discussion.

Cancers of the Breast Duct

The most commonly occurring of all the breast cancers is the scirrhous adenocarcinoma (skĭr′us ad-ĕ-no-kar-sĭ-no′mah) which accounts for nearly 80 percent of all breast cancers. It arises from the mammary duct–lining cells, most commonly occurring at or near menopause. The term *scirrhous*—which means hard—refers to the great amount of fibrous scar tissue that usually surrounds and supports these tumors, giving them a hard, grainy texture. Such cancers develop most often in the upper, outer portion of the breast (Figure 5) and grow relatively slowly, doubling their size every two to nine months.

If we consider that a cancerous lump grows from a single abnormal cell—with one cell dividing to become two, two to become four and so on—growth to the size of just one centimeter (about that of a large green pea) would take thirty such divisions. Even the fastest-growing of these cancers would require at least five years to reach that size; the slowest ones, as long as twenty years. The long growth phase—before the cancer has even

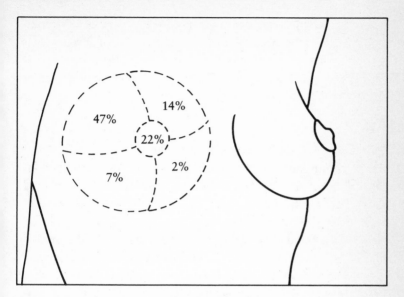

Figure 5. Distribution of cancers by location.

reached detectable size by palpation (touch) or mammography—makes control of cancer-promoting risk factors and vigilant routine examination all during a woman's life even more important.

Very early in their course, these cancers may be confined to the duct-lining cells, not having crept into the deeper layers of tissue. Specialists label cancers at this stage "carcinoma in situ," which means that no spread—even microscopically—has yet occurred. This early, noninfiltrative stage will over time usually give way to some degree of invasion and the cancer then becomes *infiltrative*.

Doctors speak of *local spread* of the cancer when it invades other types of tissue nearby (such as the skin of the breast or muscles of the chest wall). When the cancerous cells leave the immediate area of the lump and travel to distant organs (the lungs, liver, bones, and brain are the most commonly affected) then the cancer has become *metastatic*. The stage of development the cancer has reached dictates prognosis and treatment to a large extent. Chapter 6 will explain treatment options for breast cancers at various stages of development.

Cancer of the Lobules (Glandular Tissue)

Less commonly, cancer arises in the milk-producing (glandular) cells of the lobules and lobes. These cancers—the kind most often seen in premenopausal women—frequently arise in both breasts or in multiple spots within one breast. Lobular carcinomas found very early in their course can also be termed *in situ*—again, meaning that no invasion of even a microscopic degree has yet occurred. You will recall from chapter 2 that these cancers exhibit a strong familial link in first-degree relatives, behave more aggressively, metastasize sooner, and usually do not respond as readily to antiestrogen drugs. Women who have a family risk for developing this kind of cancer require close follow-up with more frequent examinations and mammograms.

Paget's Disease of the Nipple

The nipple can develop a different kind of cancer called Paget's disease—usually in older women. Although this kind of cancer represents a fair percentage of all breast tumors, it bears greater likeness to skin cancer than to breast cancer. Microscopically, it is a cancerous growth of the epidermal layer (uppermost layer) of the skin, and may remain confined to the skin alone. Often, however, close to the nipple in the ducts leading to it, a small ductal cancer will arise simultaneously. Sources disagree about whether Paget's disease should be called a skin invasion by an underlying ductal cancer, or whether it represents merely a skin cancer of the nipple.

The earliest signs of Paget's disease are persistent redness, scaliness, burning, and itching of the nipple. Later the nipple may enlarge and even crack and weep to form a crusty area. Finally, the area of involved skin may ulcerate.

If the cancer remains confined to the skin of the nipple only, prognosis for cure after surgical removal of the cancerous tissue is quite good. Again, as with other cancers of the breast, early detection and treatment improve your chances of beating the disease. Once the cancer has spread to nearby lymph nodes, chances for cure drop significantly.

The Cardinal Warning Signs of Breast Cancer

Remember, delaying discovery of a breast cancer only makes a cure more difficult. See your doctor if you note any of the following symptoms:

- The appearance of a new lump in your breast or armpit.
- Your nipple retracts or turns inside (when it was formerly normal).
- A change in the size or shape of your breasts apart from normal monthly patterns.
- A change in the color or feel of the skin of your breast or nipple (such as dimpling, puckering, redness, or scaling).
- A discharge from your nipple.

Questions and Answers

Here are answers to some commonly asked questions about changes in breast tissue.

Q: I found a lump in my underarm that was tender. It seemed
    to come up rather quickly and frightened me. I was almost
    too afraid to go to the doctor for fear of what it might be,
    but finally I did. My doctor told me I had a sebaceous cyst
    and put me on antibiotics. It has gone down, but I can still
    feel a little knot. Could my doctor have been wrong?

A: Your doctor is most likely absolutely correct. Sebaceous
    cysts, which occur quite commonly, can develop anywhere
    on the body; they tend to form most often in the groin,
    under the arm, and on the back of the neck. The sudden
    appearance of a tender often red area in the axilla (under-
    arm) usually turns out to be a cyst.

The sebaceous cyst develops when the neck of one of the oil-
producing glands (that lubricate the skin) becomes clogged. The
gland continues to produce the oil (or sebum), and because the
oil cannot exit through the neck of the gland, it backs up. After
a time, the pressure from the amount of sebum in the gland shuts
off further oil production. The clogged gland may remain quiet
in this state for a long period of time. At some point, however,
bacteria may wend their way down into the gland and start an
infection. Very quickly the gland becomes swollen and tender.
Left untended, it may spontaneously rupture and drain pus.
Reached in time with antibiotics, the infection can clear up and
the swelling subside, leaving a smaller nontender "knot." The
only way to get rid of the knot forever is to surgically remove
it. Your physician can do this for you if you like. Because breast
cancers often spread to lymph nodes in this area, you were
prudent to have your doctor check out the lump. And although
the chances of this kind of lump being cancerous is very small,
should the knot remain unchanged or grow, you should certainly
have it rechecked by your doctor.

Q: My fourteen-year-old son has developed a swollen, tender
    breast. This breast is obviously larger than his other one.

There is breast cancer in the family. Is it possible that he could have breast cancer?

A: It would be quite unusual for so young a person—male or female—to develop breast cancer even with a strong family history. But the situation demands the attention of a physician. The commonest cause of such swelling is a condition called *gynecomastia,* which frequently afflicts teenage boys. Surges in reproductive hormones seen at puberty in both sexes most likely cause this problem, and it usually subsides on its own. Local measures, such as the application of heat and low doses of anti-inflammatory pain medication, may be all that the doctor prescribes initially. If the swelling persists, your doctor will no doubt need to carry out a more extensive evaluation (breast biopsy, etc.) to be certain of the cause.

Q: My thirteen-year-old daughter is developing enormous breasts. I don't just mean large, but so huge that she has difficulty finding any clothing to fit her. She is quite embarrassed about this problem. They seem to be the same size, but I am concerned that something might be wrong. Could this be breast cancer?

A: What you describe is the relatively uncommon condition of *virginal hypertrophy* of the breasts. At puberty, the surges of female hormone normally stimulate the growth of breast tissue. Occasionally, this process fails to turn off at the appropriate time and huge breasts—sometimes weighing as much as forty pounds or more—develop. As opposed to the gynecomastia seen in young boys, virginal hypertrophy does not spontaneously go away. Only plastic surgery to reduce the size of the breasts can correct the problem. As to increased risk for breast cancer, although size alone would make early detection by examination difficult, the greatest problem for these young women is a cosmetic one.

Your daughter should certainly see her doctor for an evaluation.

Q: I am breast-feeding my baby, and I have noticed many new lumps in my breast. Is this normal?

A: Sometimes, during active milk production, one or more of the ducts leading to the nipple can occlude, creating cystic pockets of milk. The new lumps may be nothing more than this. Occasionally, however, these pockets become infected (by bacteria introduced from the baby's mouth through nursing) and the lump becomes red, warm, and tender. This condition—mastitis—usually requires antibiotics and local application of warm packs. Any newly developed lump should be examined by your doctor, because breast cancers can and do arise during pregnancy and in the postpartum (after delivery) period.

6

If Diagnosed, the Outlook for Recovery

I have included this chapter on treatment and recovery for several reasons: First, I want to help you unravel the worlds of medical and surgical oncology (the cancer treatment specialties) and give you information on currently available methods of treating breast cancer. Second, there may be some readers who may now have or perhaps have had breast cancer or know someone who does—a mother, grandmother, aunt, sister, daughter, or friend. Those readers will both want and need such information.

The material I present here is designed to inform you, not to alarm you. It will help you make sense of the prescribed treatments you, your relative, or friend may undergo, and acquaint you with the specialist physicians who may be involved. You will also learn a little about what *you* can do to help promote a healing state of mind. Should you or a friend or relative ever have to face the disease, I think this information will be of benefit.

Stages of Breast Cancers

Many states require by law that the physicians inform a cancer patient of *all* available treatment options. The National Cancer Institute Cancer Information Service (available toll-free by telephone at 1–800–4–CANCER) or your local chapter of the American Cancer Society can tell you if your state requires physicians to do so. It is the patient who must in the end decide which method of treatment she wishes to have, and to do this, she may want to seek a second or even a third opinion about her case. Most insurance companies will pay the cost of second opinions, and many even require them before they will cover the cost of surgical procedures. Above all, however, a woman should feel at ease with the treatment plan she chooses and confident in the abilities of the medical team who will carry it out.

Prognosis and treatment of breast cancer—or any cancer for that matter—depends largely on the extent to which the cancerous cells have invaded healthy tissues. Survival rates, measured as the percent of patients still alive and well five years after the cancer has been found and treated, vary greatly depending not only on the kind of cancer, but also on the stage of the cancer at the time action is taken. Specialists divide breast cancer into the following five stages based on the degree of spread that has occurred at the time of diagnosis. Because the stage of the cancer dictates, in part, which treatment options would be most effective, I will also refer to these stages later when I discuss the various medical and surgical options available.

Carcinoma *in Situ*

These cancers can often only be detected on a mammogram, because they may not yet even have reached the size at which they can be felt. The tumor has not spread beyond the boundaries of the milk duct–lining cells.

- PROGNOSIS FOR CURE AT THIS STAGE: Greater than 95 percent

Stage I

Breast cancers of this stage are beyond the stage of the *in situ* type, but they're still smaller than two centimeters in size (an inch or less) and there has not been any spread to lymph nodes (or glands).

- PROGNOSIS FOR CURE AT THIS STAGE: About 85 percent

Stage II

These tumors are still only about two centimeters in size, but *have* spread to the lymph nodes under the arm. This designation also applies to slightly larger tumors, between two and five centimeters (between one and two inches), which have not yet spread to the lymph nodes.

- PROGNOSIS FOR CURE AT THIS STAGE: About 65 percent

Stage III

The cancerous lump has reached five centimeters or larger and may have invaded the tissues of the chest wall, overlying skin or the lymph glands farther away than the armpit.

- PROGNOSIS FOR CURE AT THIS STAGE: About 40 percent

Stage IV

This stage refers to cancer that has widely metastasized (spread) to other parts of the body (lungs, liver, bone, brain, etc.)

- PROGNOSIS FOR CURE AT THIS STAGE: About 10 percent

You can easily see the strikingly adverse impact of delay in diagnosis; the prognosis for cure drops from more than 95 percent in the breast cancers caught earliest to only about 10 percent in those tumors that have already spread to distant sites.

If any woman ever needs hard evidence that awareness, early diagnosis, and early treatment of breast cancer are critically important, the preceding statistics should certainly be enough.

The Medical and Surgical Oncology Team

A disease as complex and varied as breast cancer requires the cooperation of a number of physicians with different areas of special expertise in oncology—the specialty dealing with the diagnosis and treatment of cancers. Because the idea of being the focus of an assembly of specialist physicians can be a little frightening or confusing to a woman with breast cancer, and her family as well, let me take a moment to acquaint you with some of the specialists who may take part in the team approach to treatment of this disease:

The Primary Care Doctor. This is the local family doctor or personal physician, the gynecologist, or an internal medicine specialist who handles your general health care. Often (especially in the case of the family doctor or internist) this physician will not only be the person a woman turns to initially to evaluate a lump, but sometimes will act as the manager of the overall treatment. The primary care doctor will often recommend the other medical and surgical specialist who will evaluate her case and explain what her options will be in following through on their recommendations.

The Surgeon. The physician who will evaluate the lump to determine if the biopsy is necessary and then actually perform the biopsy and any mastectomy or lumpectomy surgery is the surgeon. In place of the primary care doctor, the surgeon will often be the specialist overseeing the case and consulting with other specialists as their services are needed.

The Anesthesiologist. The anesthesiologist is responsible for making certain a woman is physically able to undergo surgery, for putting her to sleep during the surgery, and for waking her up safely afterward.

The Pathologist. The physician who analyzes the cancerous tissue under the microscope and actually makes the diagnosis of the type and extent of the cancer removed on biopsy or surgery is the pathologist. Those of us in medicine refer to this kind of physician (along with a few other subspecialties) as a "doctor's doctor." By this, I mean that other doctors rely on the knowledge and clinical skill of the pathologists to guide treatment decisions. Very likely, a breast cancer patient will never meet the pathologists on her oncology team, but their role is absolutely essential.

These tissue doctors will examine the tumor specimen in a

variety of ways, using special staining techniques for study under the microscope and the electron microscope, to determine a number of factors on which decisions regarding treatment will hinge.

Among these factors are what kind of cancer it is, how abnormal and aggressive the cells appear, whether the tumor has invaded the normal tissues nearby or the lymph nodes, and, especially important to treatment, whether the cancer cells possess hormone receptors on their surfaces that would allow them to respond to hormone therapy. These receptors, which are peculiar to breast cancers, function in a lock-and-key fashion with the female reproductive hormones (both estrogen and progesterone). The receptor (the lock) is nothing more than an area on the surface of the tumor cell that has a shape or configuration that "fits" the shape of the hormone (the key).

Tumors with a large number of these receptors—designated *hormone receptor positive*—respond better to treatment with the new antihormone drugs, such as Tamoxifen. Better response promotes better tumor cell killing, which means better survival rates. Specialists refer to tumors with few of the receptors present on the surface as *receptor negative*.

The more aggressive nature of cancers in premenopausal women and the poorer survival rates of black women with breast cancer may be connected in some way with the fact that tumors in these patients usually have fewer hormone receptors, i.e., they are receptor negative. Oncologists rely on adjuvant chemotherapy (treatment with drugs following removal of a tumor), instead of antihormones to combat these tumors.

The Medical Oncologist.   The medical oncologist specializes in the treatment of cancers by chemotherapy, which is the use of cytotoxic (cell-killing) drugs, hormones, or antihormones. The medical oncologist may become involved at the outset of treatment (from the time biopsy proves a lump to be a cancer) or may join the oncology team after the patient has already had surgery and radiation and administer adjuvant chemotherapy.

The Radiation Oncologist.   The medical doctor who has specialized first in radiology (diagnosing diseases with X rays) and then has had further extensive training in cancer treatment by X ray is the radiation oncologist. This physician will be responsible for recommending, designing the plan for, and supervising or administering cancer treatment with X ray or cobalt implants should this be necessary. A further discussion of radiation therapy can be found later in this chapter.

The Plastic Surgeon.   The plastic surgeon is a surgical specialist responsible for reconstructing the breast to a near normal size and shape after mastectomy should mastectomy prove necessary.

Some of these doctors will have greater roles than others in any particular cancer treatment. Because many heads are usually better than one, a patient can expect the best medical and surgical advice in treatment planning when the group works together as a team. Many large hospitals expand on this approach—particularly for complicated cancer cases—by bringing the case for open discussion at regularly held assemblies of cancer specialists. The one in our area—called the Tumor Board—meets weekly, with doctors from all eight area hospitals in attendance to offer their insight, input, or advice on how best to approach a case.

Methods of Treating Breast Cancers

In the treatment of breast cancer—as with any other disease—there is probably no single *right* way, because each woman and each breast cancer is unique. In light of these differences, a number of approaches to treatment exist, which can be used individually or in concert to provide the greatest chance for curing the disease in a particular woman. The main modes of treatment fall into three broad groupings: surgery, radiation, and chemotherapy (including hormone treatment). Let's take them one at a time.

Surgery

Mastectomy (Breast Removal)

As far back as ancient Rome, physicians recognized that removal of a cancerous breast in some cases improved a woman's survival of the disease, and in those early times, physicians performed a surgical procedure to remove the breast tissue (what modern surgeons would call a simple mastectomy). Surgical removal of a cancerous breast still remains the cornerstone of treatment, although nowadays, improvements in radiation and chemotherapy have made the extent of breast removal required for cure less drastic if the cancer is discovered early. There are several degrees of mastectomy.

Radical Mastectomy. The most extensive procedure (developed by a famous surgeon named Halsted and often called Halsted's operation in his honor) involves the removal of the entire breast, the overlying skin, the chest wall muscles (pectoral muscles) underneath the breast, and all the lymph nodes or glands and fat in the armpit on that side. This procedure remained the standard of treatment of breast cancer for nearly seventy-five years. Because of the chest wall disfigurement, arm swelling, and arm weakness that often followed this procedure, modern cancer surgeons rarely—if ever—perform the radical mastectomy. Today's surgeons opt instead for less extensive surgeries that offer equally good chances for cure with fewer problems.

Modified Radical Mastectomy. In this operation, the surgeon again removes all the breast tissue, some skin overlying the cancer (including the nipple and surrounding areola), as well as the lymph glands in the armpit; however, this operation requires removal of only the layer of tissue covering the chest wall muscles, sparing the muscles themselves. After the surgery, women find much less swelling of the arm, and usually recover their arm strength fully with physical therapy. Because the chest muscles remain to give the chest wall its normal contour, reconstructive breast surgery (returning the breast to near normal shape, size, and appearance through plastic surgery and artificial breast implants) can be done more easily after this operation. If the cancer has spread to the lymph glands, doctors will usually recommend additional therapy with hormones, chemotherapy, or radiation (X rays) to improve the odds for cure.

Simple Mastectomy. Here, the surgeon removes only the breast and occasionally a sampling of a few lymph nodes very close to the breast to check for spread. However, taking only a sample of those lymph nodes closest to the breast can mean the spread of cancer to other nearby lymph nodes could be missed; for this reason, some doctors will recommend that women who choose simple mastectomy have radiation (X-ray) therapy afterward—even if none of the sample of lymph nodes showed spread of the cancer. This less extensive surgical approach does have a number of pluses: After surgery, because the armpit has been for the most part undisturbed, arm swelling usually does not occur. Also, because the muscles of the arm and chest remain as they were, women suffer no loss of arm strength after this operation and breast reconstruction is quite easy to accomplish.

Breast-Conserving Surgeries

Advances in adjuvant (additional) therapy with cancer-killing drugs, hormones, and radiation have in recent years resulted in a less drastic method of treatment of the earliest stages of breast cancer: carcinoma *in situ* and stages I and II. A woman who discovers her breast cancer in these early stages may now opt (with the guidance of her medical and surgical team) for a lesser surgery that will save most or virtually all of her breast without worsening her odds for surviving the cancer.

Partial Mastectomy.   In this least extensive of all the mastectomies, the surgeon removes only the pie-shaped segment of breast tissue containing the cancerous lump itself and the overlying skin. The operation leaves the remainder of the breast— including the nipple and areola—intact. To check for spread of the cancer, the surgeon may remove some of the lymph glands in the armpit through a separate incision. A word of caution about this procedure is warranted, however, in light of recently released research from Japan. The Japanese study (Suchiro, S., et. al., *Surgery, Gynecology, and Obstetrics,* 1989) has indicated that as many as 37 percent of the women who underwent modified radical mastectomy with early cancers (i.e., those who might have been candidates for a breast-conserving surgery) proved to have microscopic invasion of the nipple and areola when the pathologist examined the specimens after surgery, even though there were no outwardly visible signs of cancerous invasion. Had these women chosen partial mastectomy and preserved their nipple and areola, cancer would have recurred. Cancers in younger women (premenopausal cancers) in particular seemed to invade the nipple earlier. A finding that one-third of these women had microscopic nipple invasion makes the consideration of postsurgical radiation or chemotherapy—which most oncology teams will recommend—even more important, and in fact, a study supported by the National Cancer Institute showed only a 15 percent recurrence rate if women were treated with postoperative chemotherapy or radiation.

Lumpectomy.   This procedure, which should only be considered for very small, very early breast tumors, amounts to little more from a surgical standpoint than an open breast biopsy. The surgeon removes only the lump itself and the smallest amount possible of overlying skin. Even in the earliest of cases, radiation therapy (or chemotherapy) should probably accompany this kind of conservative approach. Based on the recent data from the National Cancer Institute (cited above) some specialists now feel comfortable using this approach. They will recommend mastectomy at a later time for the 15 percent of women who suffer recurrence of their cancer after lumpectomy plus radiation or chemotherapy—thus sparing the breasts of the 85 percent of women whose cancers do not recur.

Safety Precautions to Take after Surgery

Most women experience some pain, swelling, and a little bruising at the site of even the least of the surgeries, and certainly, the more extensive the operation, the greater these side effects will be. Healing the surgical wounds takes time—perhaps two or three weeks for the incision to heal and the bruising to fade and local swelling to leave. It may take up to two years for the scars to mature and fade to their fullest extent.

After the more extensive removal of the axillary (armpit) lymph nodes, arm swelling may be a more persistent problem. To prevent any postoperative problems, a woman must take meticulous care of her arm and hand on the side of the surgery. Here are some of the precautions she would probably want to take in this regard:

- Avoid wearing tight watchbands or jewelry and nightgowns or blouses with elastic bands or tightly fitting sleeves. Do not allow injections of medication, vaccinations, TB skin tests, or blood sampling to be done in that arm, if possible; avoid having blood pressure tested on that arm as well.

- Avoid skin irritation from sunburns and cooking burns and use gloves when handling harsh chemicals or scouring compounds.

- Protect the skin from injury by never cutting cuticles (use lotions to dissolve if needed) and never gardening without heavy gloves; furthermore, use a thimble when sewing, use an electric razor to lessen the chances of nicking the armpit when shaving, and avoid insect bites and stings by using repellent when outdoors.

- Protect from infection by thoroughly washing any cut—even a small one—right away, applying an antibacterial ointment or cream, and covering with a light, loose bandage. If infection should arise (signaled by increasing redness, drainage of pus, warmth, and tenderness) it is important to contact the personal physician or surgeon right away.

Hospital Course

The length of time a breast cancer patient will spend in the hospital depends, naturally, on how extensive a surgical procedure she needs, how she fares both during and after surgery, how fit she was prior to the operation, and whether any complications arise during her stay. In most instances, a woman can undergo lumpectomy as a one-day surgical procedure, i.e., going into the hospital on the morning of surgery, having the operation, and spending one night in the hospital. A simple total mastectomy may require only a three-day hospital stay, whereas a modified radical mastectomy will usually require five days to a week after surgery to recover sufficiently.

Postoperative Emotional Concerns

As adults, we all face emotional crises in our lives, sometimes of such immense magnitude that they strain—often to the limits of our endurance—our abilities to cope with them. Confronting the death of a parent or spouse, the serious illness of a loved one, or a challenge to our own health and well-being rank among the heaviest emotional burdens all of us must at some point face.

The diagnosis of breast cancer, whether in yourself or in a friend or relative, brings with it all the normal human emotions associated with an assault on health and peace of mind: rage, anger, frustration, fear, anxiety, and frequently depression. These feelings are normal and expected under such duress, but coping with them alone may require emotional and physical reserves of strength that you simply may not have at the moment. Emotional health plays such a critical role in the ultimate recovery process that the patient and her family and friends must not let themselves neglect it.

We should never be afraid—or as in the case of some women, actually embarrassed—to seek outside help. Such help may take the form of a friend or family member with whom you can talk openly about your feelings, or you may turn to a clergyman, social worker, or counselor. A woman facing breast cancer may find talking to another woman who has been through the same trial—such as an American Cancer Society Reach to Recovery volunteer—helps her dig out from the emotional avalanche she may feel has smothered her. Remember that no woman need suffer the ravages of these fears and frustrations alone. Many hospitals maintain a staff of counselors and social workers to answer questions, allay fears, or just be good listeners.

Now, more than ever, the patient and her family must support their emotional selves. The patient should be surrounded with upbeat people, living things, flowers, sunlit rooms, pleasant colors, and humor. One of the most powerful recovery tools of all is laughter: it really *is* the best medicine. As cliché as it sounds, more and more studies prove its medical potential. Laughing—and I mean good robust belly laughing—releases certain natural painkillers; slows the release of stress hormones; and exercises the muscles of the heart, lungs, face, shoulders, and diaphragm. Perhaps through release of certain chemical messengers in the brain, laughter may be one of the best antidepressants available. Engage in a little "humor therapy" by reading the comics, watching funny movies (even slapstick such as the Marx brothers or the Three Stooges), listening to humorous stories or jokes.

Approximate Costs for Breast Cancer Surgery

Some readers may have questions about the costs of these treatments. I have looked into typical charges around the country to give you at least some idea of what to reasonably expect.

Costs throughout the United States may vary widely. The charges that I have listed here were an average range of the charges from Arkansas, New York City, San Francisco, and Florida.

Hospital charges (this does not include the surgeon's fee, which I will address later) for a typical stay, plus operating room fees and anesthesia will be approximately:

$1,000–3,000 for outpatient one-day surgery for lumpectomy
$3,500–5,000 for three-day stay for a simple total mastectomy
$5,500–8,000 for a five-day stay for the modified radical mastectomy procedure

The Surgeon's Fee. The surgeon's price for performing the operation, caring for the patient while in the hospital and afterward will depend on the extent of the procedure required.

Even though the amounts may vary in different locations around the country, a comparison of the procedures should be helpful and will at least give you some indication of relative costs. The following ranges again represent the average of the locations listed above:

$120–200 for needle biopsy of the breast
$440–580 for excision of a benign or malignant cyst (this is also about the cost of a lumpectomy)
$510–650 for partial mastectomy
$840–960 for simple or total mastectomy
$1,400–1,800 for modified radical mastectomy with lymph node dissection
$1,400–1,800 for radical mastectomy

Check with your state's insurance commission if you feel a charge is out of line. The commission should keep track of the typical rates in your area.

Breast Reconstruction after Mastectomy

In the early days of breast cancer surgery, the chest wall disfigurement caused by the radical mastectomy often left women with as many psychological, or emotional, scars as physical ones. Although from a recovery standpoint, the newer and less extensive procedures, such as the modified radical and simple mastectomies, are less traumatic, they still leave the woman without her breast. For many women the sense of loss felt after removal of the breast is not so great, and they adjust quite well to simply wearing a breast form (or prosthesis) in their brassiere for shape. Other women, however, feel less than emotionally whole after mastectomy and opt for rehabilitative surgeries to reconstruct a near-normal breast. For those of you who may wish to know more about this option, here's a brief outline of the various procedures.

Simple Implant Placement.   If you, your friend, or relative has undergone a simple mastectomy or modified radical mastectomy, which preserve the muscular structure of the chest wall, a plastic surgeon alone can insert a silicon breast implant to restore a normal shape to the breast area. This easy operation can be performed either at the time of the mastectomy (which some surgeons prefer) or later as an outpatient or one-day surgical procedure *after* radiation and chemotherapy. The only requirement is that the woman's chest wall have sufficient good-quality skin to cover the implant—which may not be the case if the tumor had inflammed or invaded the skin or was quite large.

Tissue Expansion.   When larger amounts of overlying skin must be removed at the initial surgery, the skin covering the chest wall may be very tight and not accommodating to placement of a breast implant beneath it. In this case, the plastic surgeon can first place a temporary expander (a kind of deflated fluid bag) under the skin and muscle. Then over the next two to three months, the patient returns to the plastic surgeon's office to have the expander gradually inflated with additional fluid. Over time, the tissues across the chest wall stretch, and when they have done so enough to accommodate the size of the implant, the woman can undergo a second operation to place the permanent implant.

Nipple Reconstruction.   Although many women feel satisfied with simply reconstructing a normal breast shape, surgeons have taken the rehabilitation process a step further in the development of plastic surgical procedures to recreate an even more normal appearing breast with a nipple and areola.

In this operation, the surgeon takes a small circle of skin, usually from the upper inside part of the thigh, and moves it to the center of the new breast. Skin moved from this area darkens after transplanting on the breast, and the color change more closely mimics the darker skin of the areola. A small piece of earlobe cartilage can serve as the nipple protrusion, with the overall effect looking quite amazingly natural.

Tissue Transfers.   When a woman has undergone more extensive surgery—such as a radical mastectomy because of muscle invasion by the cancer—the shape of the chest wall changes. To restore a normal-looking breast in these cases, the chest wall muscles must be replaced. This operation may sound impossible, but accomplished plastic surgeons can quite easily borrow flaps of muscle and skin from other areas—such as the latissimus dorsi muscle group on the back, behind the arm, and by the shoulder blade or the rectus abdominus group on the lower abdomen—where their loss will be less noticeable. The surgeon then moves the flap to reshape the chest contour. After the woman has recovered from this first stage operation, she can undergo placement of a breast implant, if needed, or nipple and areola reconstruction. Because of their more extensive surgical nature, tissue-transfer procedures usually require a hospital stay of a week or so.

Approximate Costs for Reconstructive Procedures

In addition to daily hospital room costs, operating room, and anesthesia charges (which will vary by location and length of stay required), the surgeon charges in the neighborhood of $1,800 to $2,000 to perform the first stage in major breast reconstruction, which would be flap rotation. The second stage, with placement of the implant (or initial placement of the implant in women who do not require the flap rotation) will cost about $950 to $1,200.

Many insurance carriers view reconstructive breast surgery after a mastectomy as a rehabilitative procedure rather than simply a cosmetic one and consequently will cover many of these costs.

Radiation Therapy

The discovery of radiation as a medical tool by Marie Curie in the 1800s forever altered the face of diagnostic medical science. The many uses of X rays in medicine, from its humble beginnings as primarily a means to see fractures and abnormal growth of our bones and infections in our lungs, has, in modern times expanded to include not only the diagnosis of many medical and surgical conditions quickly and painlessly but, as I have already said, the treatment of many cancers.

In the case of breast cancer, the radiation oncologist is most often called on to use X-ray therapy as an additional margin of safety after surgery has been done to remove the tumor. This method of radiation therapy uses the X rays to eradicate any rogue cancer cells that may still linger in the area where the lump has been or in the neighboring lymph nodes. In some cases, the oncology team may recommend the use of radiation therapy alone (i.e., without surgery) as the best choice of treatment.

Radiation oncologists can administer the cancer-destroying X-ray dosage in two ways. In either of these methods, the precise amount of radiation needed and the time of exposure required to destroy the cancer depend on the size of the tumor, the extent to which it has spread, and the type of cancer it is. Radiation therapy can be administered externally or internally.

External Radiation.   For this procedure, a machine "beams" high-energy radiation (or X rays) at the areas that contain the cancerous tissues: the lump area, the lymph nodes of the armpit, and those near the breastbone. This kind of radiation therapy involves administering small doses of X rays directly to these sites on a regular schedule (usually Monday through Friday for about twenty to twenty-five minutes a day over a period of several weeks [often four or five]. Over time, the dose of radiation delivered to the area adds up to a cancer-killing dose of 4,400 to 5,000 rads (which stands for the radiation absorbed dose). Giving the dose in small daily increments instead of all at once results in fewer side effects (the precise nature of which I will discuss in detail shortly). In most cases, a week or two after a woman has completed her initial series of X-ray treatments, her doctor may recommend another *booster dose* of concentrated radiation to the breast lump area over a five- to ten-day period.

Although this method of radiation treatment requires a month or more of near daily trips to the hospital, the actual amount of time spent taking treatments is relatively small. Because the therapy is an outpatient procedure, a woman's life—both business and social—can go on in a nearly normal fashion within the confines of how she feels. Some women tolerate the effects of radiation therapy better than others.

Internally Implanted Radiation. The second method of administration involves surgically implanting radioactive material directly into the breast. In the operating room while the patient is asleep, the surgeon inserts slender hollow plastic tubes through the skin into the area where the tumor is (or was). Once she is safely back to a private room, the radiation oncologist inserts the dose of radiation (usually the isotope iridium) through the plastic tubing, where it is left for a specified amount of time. The radioactive implant then emits small continuous doses of radiation right at the site of the tumor. During the following two or three days that the treatment implant is in place, her breast will be slightly radioactive, and this radiation could pose a slight risk to visitors as well as the medical personnel who care for her. Therefore, for the duration of treatment, she would have to remain in the hospital, and family, friends, and even the nursing staff would have to keep their time spent with her to a minimum. Her doctor will not discharge her from the hospital until the surgeon removes the implant, and the risk of exposing others to the radiation is past.

Radiation Side Effects

Many women receiving radiation for breast cancer experience slight nausea, loss of appetite, hair loss, and fatigue. These symptoms may increase as the course of treatment progresses, but will resolve soon after it is finished. The skin of the radiated area may at first become red and irritated much like a sunburn, which then becomes browner, like a tan. Some patients report excessive drying of the skin during the treatments and others increased moisture.

It's important for a breast cancer patient to pay attention to nutrition, even though she might have less relish for food at this time. She needs a diet rich in quality protein (roughly 70 to 100 grams per day) from fish, meat, poultry, or dairy sources that is supplemented with fruits and vegetables. Her diet should meet the recommended daily allowance for vitamins and minerals, and she should drink plenty of fluids.

She can minimize the irritation to her skin by taking especially good care of it during and after the course of radiation. Most radiation oncologists advise against the use of deodorants, perfumed soaps or cosmetics, ointments or creams, and binding or restrictive clothing or brassieres (especially those with wires) during the course of treatment. Bathing or showering gently, using warm (not hot) water, mild soap without deodorant, and patting the skin dry with a soft cotton towel would be the best course to follow. Also, choosing loosely fitting, soft cotton or silk garments for greater comfort and protection will help.

Approximate Cost of Treatment

I discovered that there are no standard codes for what is involved in radiation therapy; such codes are necessary to calculate an average charge for this form of therapy. Any of you who would like to know specifics should contact the oncology service at your local hospital, your state's insurance commission, or your local American Cancer Society to find out the usual cost of receiving radiation therapy in your area.

Chemotherapy

Over the last thirty to thirty-five years, cancer researchers have worked diligently to develop medications that wipe out cancers, and during that time, there have been dramatic successes in cancer cure or remission through chemotherapy. Such diseases as oat cell cancer of the lung, some cancers of the testicle, and certain leukemias can be cured through the use of cancer-killing medicines alone, but not all cancers respond as well.

The first medical reports of experimental use of adjuvant chemotherapy (in addition to surgical removal of tumor) for breast cancer appeared about 1955, and at that time, only a very few cancer-killing drugs were known. Much of what medical researchers in the 1950s *did* know about the effects of cytotoxic (cell-killing) drugs on humans they had learned from the use of nitrogen mustard gas as a weapon during World War II. Year by year, through research and experimentation, other drugs with the power to kill living cells appeared, and today, by a conservative estimate, some thirty to forty such anticancer drugs are known. What began as experimental treatment, today represents the standard of cancer care, with an entire medical subspecialty—the field of medical oncology—developing around the use of these medications to combat cancers.

Although in the case of breast cancer, oncologists typically still reserve chemotherapy for use after surgery—except in Stage IV cases, which have advanced so widely that surgery may do no good—the search continues for a drug or combination of drugs that can achieve as high a cure rate as surgery.

Medical oncologists who prescribe and administer chemotherapy for treatment of breast cancer usually do so either (1) just after a woman has undergone surgical removal of the tumor (whether by mastectomy or breast-conserving operations) and has completed her course of radiation therapy to the area. The purpose of additional chemotherapy (or hormone therapy) is to clean up any microscopic metastases (tiny clusters of stray cancer cells too small to be detected), which have already migrated to distant sites. Or (2) in the event of recurrence of the cancer. Some experts recommend postponing chemotherapy until a cancer recurs because of the extreme toxicity of the drugs. There is some debate in the field of oncology about whether it really changes survival rates to administer the course of chemotherapy immediately after surgery or to reserve using the drugs only for those women whose cancers recur. You may find specialists who will recommend withholding these very toxic drugs until such time as they are needed to stop regrowth of tumor cells.

How Does Chemotherapy Kill Cancer Cells?

Most of the cell-killing drugs do their damage by preventing those cells from dividing and growing normally. This damaging, or killing, effect is not limited to cancer cells, however, but affects healthy, normal ones as well. Fortunately, normal tissues have a slight advantage in this regard. Cancer cells usually grow and divide with great abandon and, therefore, when compared to the slower-dividing rate of most normal cells of the body, at any given time a much greater proportion of cancerous cells will be in the middle of a dividing process. When a cell is at this critical point in its division it is most vulnerable to the killing effect of the cytotoxic drugs; thus each dose of the drug kills far more cancer cells than normal ones.

Not all of our normal tissues grow at such a slow rate, however. The cells that form our hair, skin, intestinal lining, and bone marrow (where our red blood cells and infection-fighting cells originate) turn over quite rapidly, to replace the millions of such cells that we shed or use up every day. These faster-growing tissues fall victim to the killing effects of anticancer drugs to a greater degree. This difference in susceptibility to damage accounts for virtually all the side effects commonly associated with chemotherapy: hair loss, nausea, vomiting, diarrhea, anemia, fatigue, and the heightened risk for infections (again, see the section on side effects for details).

Who Should Have Chemotherapy?

Although there are some general guidelines regarding who will benefit from this regimen, the final decision about whether a woman with breast cancer should have chemotherapy rests with her along with her oncology team. The recommendations that the National Cancer Institute has outlined are:

Premenopausal Women
- In whom the cancer has already spread to the lymph nodes in the armpit (even if the cancer might also respond to hormones, but especially if it would not).
- With large or aggressive tumors.
- Who developed the breast cancer during pregnancy.
- Who develop their cancer before age forty.

Postmenopausal Women
- Whose cancer has spread to the lymph nodes and who have positive hormone receptors should receive Tamoxifen (for up to five years) postoperatively.

- Whose cancer has spread to lymph nodes, but whose cancers do not have high hormone receptor levels.
- With no cancer spread to lymph nodes but who for other reasons fall into very high risk groups *may* be candidates for chemotherapy.

Chemotherapy Administration

Exact routines and regimens vary depending on the type and extent of the cancer, the health of the woman, and the oncologist in question, but in general, a multidrug approach appears to result in the best chances for destroying the cancer. The oncologist selects a regimen of several cytotoxic drugs (usually from two to five) to be given together in bursts of therapy every few (one to four) weeks for about six months in some cases to as long as four or five years for the antiestrogen, Tamoxifen.

Different anticancer drugs interrupt the growth and division of the cells at different points in the dividing process. Within the tumor, there will be cancer cells in all phases of division, so logically, hitting the cancer with a barrage of drugs simultaneously will destroy cells in several different phases. The treatment is given orally in some cases, or by injection into the muscle or intravenously while in the doctor's office.

In the treatment of breast cancer, the drugs most commonly used are 5-fluorouracil (5-FU), cyclophosphamide (Cytoxan), methotrexate (MTX), doxorubicin (Adriamycin), vincristine (Oncovin), melphalan or *L*-phenylalanine mustard (*L*-PAM). While there probably is no single *correct* regimen, two combinations of these drugs seem to work quite well together. For this reason, many women receive either the FAC regimen (which stands for 5-FU plus Adriamycin plus Cytoxan) or the CMF regimen (Cytoxan plus MTX plus 5-FU). Some specialists feel that the FAC regimen offers slightly better treatment of distant areas of the body to which the cancer has spread, but again, let me stress that there simply is no single right combination. The choice of treatment must be individualized from case to case by the oncology team specialists.

There is a new antibioticlike drug, called mitoxantrone, which can thus far only be administered in the hospital but seems to offer some good results. Although it has not yet been fully cleared by the Food and Drug Administration for use in breast cancer, it currently can be used in certain cases. However, at this point its price remains its major drawback, costing on the order of $800 to $1,000 per dose.

Most experts agree that they must hit the cancer very hard at the beginning of chemotherapy treatment and consequently must carefully calculate the largest dose their patient can tolerate. The stronger the dose your oncologist can safely administer, the greater the chances for a cure, but unfortunately, the more plagued the patient will likely be with unpleasant side effects.

Side Effects of Chemotherapy

Chemotherapeutic drugs are potent cell poisons that, as you've already read, affect healthy tissues as well as cancerous ones. Although most of these side effects may make the patient miserable and uncomfortable, once the treatment stops, the unpleasant symptoms usually stop, too. In a few instances, however, the side effects can remain. Adriamycin, for example, can cause some injury to the heart, and some of the drugs may cause sterility. The more rapidly growing tissues that I mentioned previously suffer to a greater extent, and their damage may cause some women on chemotherapy to experience (usually temporary) problems in the following areas of their bodies.

Gastrointestinal Tract. Gastrointestinal tract side effects include mouth ulcers, yeast infections of the mouth or rectal area, soreness of the tongue, nausea, vomiting, diarrhea, and loss of appetite.

Hair.   Hair thinning or in some cases temporary baldness can occur.

Blood and Bone Marrow.   Problems in this area include anemia (and the weakness and fatigue that accompany it), susceptibility to infections, difficulty clotting the blood, and even the remote possibility of later developing a second cancer (such as leukemia or lymphoma) involving the blood or bone marrow.

Reproductive Tract.   Menstrual changes ranging from heavy flow and clotting to temporary cessation of menstruation (with the latter probably occurring more frequently) are reproductive tract side effects.

Approximate Costs of Chemotherapy

Again, average prices around the country will vary for such treatments. But to give you at least some indication of the expenses involved in this portion of breast cancer treatment, I spoke with several oncology specialists.

The FAC regimen, given as an outpatient every four weeks, including the charge for the medication, its administration, and seeing the doctor each time, may cost from $400 to $500 per treatment. A typical regimen of adjuvant chemotherapy for breast cancer may continue for six cycles (in this case six months), bringing the total cost for this treatment to approximately $2,400 to $3,000.

Tamoxifen (for those tumors that are hormone receptor positive) is a much less toxic and, at least on a monthly basis, a less expensive regimen. Although administration and follow-up care during treatment with Tamoxifen may only cost $60 per month, the length of treatment is significantly longer—usually two to five years. Based on this figure, over the entire treatment, a course of Tamoxifen can range from $1,400 to $3,600.

Most insurance companies will cover all or a large portion of treatment costs for chemotherapy.

The Healing Force of the Mind

I would like to take a moment to bring up a subject I touched on in chapter 4: the importance of preventive thinking. And I would like to turn that phrase just a little to call it *curative thinking*. Perhaps you or someone you love has been stricken by breast cancer (or some other form of life-threatening illness or injury). This certainly has been the case in my own family. I have, in the last fifteen years, lost my father to severe heart disease, a grandmother to a stroke, and my mother and her three aunts to various forms of cancer. And both as a family member and a physician, I have witnessed the remarkable difference that a patient's attitude toward their disease can make.

Let me illustrate this point with an example from my own family. Two of my great aunts who died of cancer were fraternal twins. In temperament, these twins were quite different. The first—whom all considered to be the stronger, smarter, more "durable" of the two—faced all of life's challenges with a stoicism I have rarely seen matched. The second developed a more happy-go-lucky approach to life, always letting the other twin assume the burden of everything from homework to housework to financial support.

The stoic twin, who suffered lung cancer, which she obstinately ignored until it had widely metastasized, succumbed very quickly to her disease—after assuring herself that her sister would be adequately provided for. The other twin developed breast cancer, for which she underwent radical mastectomy; although during surgery, her doctors discovered that it had already spread to the tissues near her heart. Her physicians recommended a course of radiation therapy, which she decided to undergo; however, their prognosis for her recovery was quite guarded.

This twin, despite what her physicians told her about the spread of the disease and her poor prognosis, simply did not accept that she would not be cured by the surgery and cobalt. Although she complied to the letter with her doctors' recommended therapy, she was determined to continue her life precisely as it had been before—dressing up every day (pretty dress, girdle, stockings, matching shoes and handbags, a necklace and earrings) even though she no longer worked. She remained concerned about her complexion and her hair and her nails. In short, she didn't miss a beat.

She coped with her own illness by remaining steadfastly convinced that she had been cured. She lived another eight years and died quietly and painlessly from a heart rhythm problem (probably caused by the invasion of cancer).

Let me hasten to add that I do not advocate that women with breast cancer should pretend they don't have it so that it will then go away. My aunt certainly did not do that—she underwent her prescribed surgery and follow-up treatment just as her doctor ordered. She simply maintained an unrivaled good attitude about it. I told her story to illustrate what a potent ally a positive mental outlook can be in the healing process. A number of psychological researchers have developed methods of harnessing this force, and they hope to use it to better the quality of the survival time of cancer patients and improve their response to radiation therapy.

One of the centers for such research happens to be associated with the University of Arkansas Medical Sciences Campus in Little Rock (where I live and work). This group—the Health Training and Research Center—bases its methods on the Simonton Approach (developed by O. Carl Simonton, M.D., and his former wife Stephanie Matthews Simonton). These methods, termed *guided imagery*, teach patients how to create a mental picture of wellness, how to envision their body's repairing itself and destroying the cancerous remnants. Many patients who have learned these curative-thinking techniques report that they (and their families) not only seem to cope more effectively with the illness, but they withstand the effects of radiation and chemotherapy with fewer complications. Those of you who find this approach to self-assisted recovery interesting can find the address and inquiry information for the Health Training and Research Center here in Little Rock, as well as a short bibliography of available books and audiocassettes pertaining to this subject in chapter 8.

Family Support: How to Give It

When a woman develops a life-threatening illness such as breast cancer, she needs the support of her family, both physically and emotionally, more than ever. You may find yourself thrust into such a situation—perhaps with your mother, sister, or grandmother. How should you act? What should you say? What can you do to help? You must maintain a positive attitude—not a phony one, a real one.

In conversation, take your cues from the patient. If she seems to want to discuss her disease, leave yourself open to allow her to do so, directly and honestly, even if the discussion seems painful. Don't try to change the subject or put a good face on the circumstances, but try not to dwell on the negatives either. If she seems disinclined to talk about her cancer with you, respect her wishes, and don't force the issue. Talk instead about everyday things: your children, her children, sales at the mall, painting the house. If you share common hobbies, such as tennis or bridge, keep her up to date on what's happening on that front. Offer to do any outside chore that may be worrying her, such as watering her plants, caring for her pets, filling in for her at her children's school or scouting activities, taking supper to her family now and again.

When you visit her, bring laughter with you. Bright balloons, fresh flowers, a new humorous book, current magazines, new photographs, a funny story, or a good joke. Above all, don't avoid her company to avoid confronting the reality of her disease. She will need your friendship, companionship, strength, and concern before surgery, in the hospital, and during recovery.

Questions and Answers

Here are answers to some commonly asked questions about breast cancer treatment.

Q: My aunt had a breast tumor removed. It had been growing there a long time and her breast looked terrible. She had a mastectomy done, but her doctor said it wasn't cancer. How can that be?

A: The most likely cause of a visibly nasty looking breast tumor which turns out not to be cancerous is the condition known as *cystosarcoma phylloides* (sis-to-sar-ko'mah fi-lo'dēz). These tumors can be benign or malignant, and the difference between them may not be apparent except to the pathologist under the microscope. The tumors can reach enormous size and be confined totally to the breast, and in the case of the benign tumors, it is usually their size that dictates whether or not a mastectomy must be done. A benign tumor, although not cancerous, can require surgical removal if it is excessively large.

Q: I am scheduled to have radiation therapy after mastectomy.
    I am concerned about the dose of radiation to the rest of my
    body. Will the rest of my body be protected from the rays?

A: The equipment used to administer therapeutic radiation (X-
    ray treatments) as opposed to diagnostic X rays, such as
    for a broken leg or arm, has built-in safeguards that direct
    the radiation to only the area to be treated. Although the
    dose of radiation most certainly affects other tissues of the
    body (as I have discussed) the actual rays pass only through
    the outlined treatment area.

Q: I have just discovered that I may have breast cancer. I have
    a lump, but I have not gotten all the reports back yet. I do
    not want to alarm my children and have considered not
    telling them I am going into the hosptial for the biopsy.
    My husband disagrees and says that we must tell them.
    What is the best way to deal with children in this situation?

A: Honestly. Although we all want to protect our children from
    unhappiness, worry, and pain, kids are much more percep-
    tive than adults generally give them credit for being. Chil-
    dren will sense that something is wrong no matter how
    diligently you try to put on a good face, and usually they
    will blame themselves for any family problem that occurs.
    Level with your children, because at this point after all,
    even you don't know yet exactly what you are up against.
    Tell them that you have a lump that has to be taken out in
    the hospital, tell them when you will be going and how
    long you expect to be gone. Tell them also that until the
    lab tests have all been evaluated, there is no need to worry
    about you. They will worry anyway, but should you choose
    not to tell them, they will surely feel something amiss and
    not know why. You need not give them more information
    than they can understand, but do encourage their questions,
    and give them honest answers.

Q: I had a very early breast cancer removed several years ago and underwent a simple breast removal and breast implant operation at the time of the surgery. I have done very well and have kept my regular check ups with the doctor, and now I don't have to go to be checked but once every six months. Should I check my own breasts monthly? What about the side with the implant?

A: A definite yes on both counts. Regularly examining the normal breast is a must because of the chance that another cancer could arise there. Although more difficult for you to do, you should become familiar with the feel of the breast which has been reconstructed. Although there is no breast tissue on that side anymore, adjacent tissues and lymph glands could be sites for recurrence.

Q: My doctor says I need therapy with the drug Tamoxifen. What are the side effects?

A: Most women tolerate treatment with Tamoxifen very well. Because it is an antihormone, women may experience symptoms associated with low hormone levels, such as hot flashes and emotionalness (sudden crying spells, irritability, and mood swings). If these effects occur, they usually disappear after completing the treatment. Long-term side effects also appear to be minimal.

Q: If I lose my hair after chemotherapy, will it grow back?

A: Yes. Usually, after any serious illness, major surgery, or assault on the hair-growing cells by anticancer drugs or radiation, hair growth stops. The hair follicle becomes dormant, and that hair shaft (the hair itself) will never be reactivated. Later when a new hair shaft begins to develop, it pushes the old dormant one out. In the case of chemotherapy or radiation, the loss may be massive or total, but is usually temporary.

7

Medical Frontiers
in Treatment

None of us can say with certainty what lies ahead, where we will be, or what we will be doing ten, five, or even one year down the road. And while there is no greater degree of certainty in medicine, recent technological developments have paved the way for promising new weapons in the war on cancer and greater hope for future generations. Although at present we consider these weapons to be only experimental work, they may become standard medical care for our children. So let's take a look at a few of these newly reported discoveries and at the impact they may have on the future.

On the Medical Frontier

In recent years and particularly since the recognition and epi-demic spread of the AIDS virus, the role of the human immune system in cancers and other diseases has received a wealth of medical research money and time. In the case of AIDS, a cata-strophic virus-induced failure of the immune system causes sus-ceptibility to diseases that could be easily dealt with by normally active immune defenses.

The normal immune system defends us from whatever it per-ceives as not being part of us (whether it be another living or-ganism, such as a bacterium or virus, or a transplanted heart or kidney). The complex recognition, relay, and destroy functions of the immune cells (most of which are of the white blood cell type) hinge on one critical factor: the tiny differences in *cell surface markers* by which they can identify and separate their own body's tissues from others. These surface markers are usu-ally protein molecules that protrude from the membrane of the cells, functioning like name tags, telling the immune fighters what cells are *us* and what are *them*.

Every moment of every day, we depend on the vigilance of our immune system to protect us from invasion by *them:* infec-tious viruses, bacteria, and fungi. Another equally critical role of the immune system, however, is to recognize, seek out, and destroy those few cells—among the billions of our body's normal cells—that have for whatever reason gone haywire, have lost their normal controls, and have become cancerous. When a lapse in this cancer early warning system occurs, a cancerous growth may find the opportunity to develop. And as we have seen, it may enjoy our unwitting assistance through the promoting effect of the many environmental risk factors over which we have control.

The cell surface markers of a person's cancer cells are slightly different from those of their "normal" cells. Recently, medical researchers have attempted to play on these minute differences to actively enlist the aid of the immune system as an ally in the war on cancer. These methods—at this point at least—are still considered experimental. Only through repeated trials (giving the treatment experimentally and monitoring the results) will we know which—if any—of these treatments will prove to be effective against breast cancer.

Antibody Cloning

Some research laboratories have begun to use the tumor cells in a slightly different way. *In vitro* tests (meaning conducted in the laboratory in a culture dish, test tube, flask, etc., as opposed to in the human body) have shown that normal immune fighter cells, when presented with tumor cells, will produce antibodies (cell-killing proteins) directed specifically against that tumor. This phenomenon is far from new or experimental, but is in fact, the basis for such mundane doctor's office diagnostic tools as the blood and urine pregnancy tests as well as throat cultures for mononucleosis and strep throat. Antibody cloning has also given us many now-standard medical treatments in regard to other kinds of diseases; for example, snake bite antivenin and the tetanus, hepatitis, and other immune globulins that can grant temporary immunity to patients who have been exposed to these substances. Applying this knowledge to laboratory production of anticancer antibodies is only a small step further in principle.

Scientists studying the cancer-destroying power of immune cells hope someday to be able to take the actual cancer cells from a patient, place them into a laboratory flask with antibody-producing white blood cells, and "grow" a batch of anticancer antibodies that will—when injected back into the patient—seek out and destroy the cancer cells wherever they may hide. Techniques similar to this one, while still deemed experimental, may already be available in some areas. If you would like more information on cancer research hospitals that may be involved in such therapy trials at present or in the near future, the National Cancer Institute resource listing in chapter 8 would be the best place for you and your physician to begin.

Interferon

Our immune system fighting cells have another weapon that they produce and unleash on cancers (and infections of certain types). This substance, identified in the 1960s, is called interferon, and it seems to exert its cancer-killing effect by actively recruiting and drawing to the area those types of immune cell that can best destroy the cancer. Researchers had high hopes that interferon would prove to be the cancer panacea, but research trials have so far disappointed them. The research goes on, however, and many medical researchers feel we have only begun to discover information about this native protein. It can now be "grown" or produced in a laboratory setting in very small (and quite expensive) quantities for use in selected cancer studies. Researchers and physicians would still consider interferon in its infancy as a cancer therapy, and availability of the substance limits its use to only a few cancer research hospitals. Your physician—through the National Cancer Institute's Physician Data Query (PDQ)—can check into locations and availability of this and other such experimental protocols. See chapter 8 for details of how to contact PDQ.

Mammastatin

Researchers at the University of Michigan announced recently that they have isolated and identified another naturally occurring body protein—dubbed mammastatin—that is present in high concentrations in normal breast tissue, but in very low levels in cancerous breast tissue. The breasts of some women exhibit extremely high concentrations of this substance—on the order of eighty times greater levels—than those found in breast cancer cells.

Scientists studying the protein have applied it to breast cancer cells in the laboratory, and it stops their growth. The beauty of its action lies in the fact that mammastatin will attach only to breast cancer cells and will not damage or kill healthy cells. As I have discussed, sparing healthy cells would be a major advantage over most of the chemotherapeutic agents now in use.

Very high estrogen levels—such as those found during pregnancy—release mammastatin. The association between pregnancy and the production of beneficial mammastatin may offer a clue as to why childless women suffer higher breast cancer rates. Much more study will doubtlessly be needed to evaluate what other triggers may stimulate the release of mammastatin, or conversely, prevent or limit its release. While great hope for future generations attends such a discovery, it will certainly be a few years before we can expect any significant medical use of this intriguing substance in prevention or treatment of breast cancer.

Securing Your Future:
Making a Commitment to Health

The goals of this book were to inform, to guide, and to motivate you. By virtue of the fact that you have chosen to read this book, you have exhibited a concern for your future. If you have learned something on an intellectual level about assessing your personal and family risk for the disease, about the many environmental promoters of breast cancer, about the types of breast cancer and the treatment choices available, then you have benefited from the first goal. If you have recognized the importance of prevention through early detection of breast cancer, then you have benefited from the second goal of this book. If, in addition, those of you in high-risk families can now truly understand the value of beginning prevention early by teaching your daughters and nieces the importance of proper diet and of avoiding those habits that might promote cancer growth, then the third goal has been reached. And if my words have been able to motivate you to take some positive action to lessen your risk for breast cancer, however large or small it may be, then I have succeeded in the most important part of my job: moving you to seize responsibility for your own health and well-being.

No one else can do the job. Only you. If you increase your breast cancer risk because you are overweight, there is no one else who can take off the pounds, no one else who can choose what you eat. If you smoke, no one can stop you from lighting up and taking that next puff, except you. If you have been diligent in making your six-month appointment to get your teeth cleaned, but neglected to schedule your annual breast exam and mammogram, there is no one else who can take your place. You can and must take control of your future.

Through research, medicine is winning the war against several cancers: Hodgkin's lymphoma, oat cell cancer of the lung, and certain of the childhood leukemias, to name but a few. And what of our war against the biggest cancer killer of women—breast cancer? The future looks brighter than ever before for ourselves and our daughters, not only in regard to finding better and less-toxic treatments for breast cancer but in finding better screening tools to determine which women carry the greatest risk for developing it and more sensitive tests to detect the cancers in all women sooner.

In some areas, the future has already arrived. The month before I finished this book, the *New England Journal of Medicine* announced that researchers have isolated a substance—called haptoglobin related protein—that appears to predict, with a high degree of reliability, which women are likely to suffer a recurrence of their breast cancer. These women, even with very early tumors (which have not even spread to the lymph nodes) could be treated with adjuvant chemotherapy and radiation, or even with prophylactic (i.e., preventative) mastectomy of the other breast, to preclude recurrence. Although this substance is still under scrutiny, it may not be long before physicians have access to this medical tool (and others like it) and will then be able, through simple blood-testing or tissue-typing techniques, to pick out those women at highest risk for developing breast cancer, who, therefore, warrant especially close and careful scrutiny.

Also, as scientists continue to evaluate the causative and promoting effects of the various environmental factors in the development of breast cancer, medical science will develop an even sharper profile of the woman at risk. Based on this ever-expanding knowledge base, the physicians of tomorrow will be able to give women even clearer and more definite advice about what they and their daughters should be doing to lessen their risk for this disease. Stay tuned, as they say on the news, for further developments.

Remember, too, that prevention through early detection gives you the edge against this killer, so don't neglect the importance of monthly breast self-examination, regular physician examination, and routine mammography after age thirty-five (or even twenty-five for the highest risk women). Begin today to assess your personal and family risk for developing breast cancer, and if you have found that you fit the breast cancer description, begin today to change your profile, to make yourself a less likely target. Take stock of all those environmental risk factors you can eliminate or change and take positive steps to effect those changes and to reduce your risk. It's up to you. Begin today.

8

Resources

Cancer Treatment Information

Availability of New Treatments

Cancer Information Service
Office of Cancer Communications
National Cancer Institute
Bethesda, MD 20892

in the continental United States (800) 4–CANCER
in Hawaii (808) 524–1234 (on Oahu)
in Alaska (800) 638–6070
in Quebec (514) 5–CANCER
in Ontario (416) 387–1153

This telephone information service also offers trained specialist staff members who speak Spanish for daytime callers in the following states: Texas, California, New York, New Jersey, Georgia, Illinois, and Florida.

General Information about Breast Cancer

Many national, state, and local groups offer free publications, pamphlets, even books about breast cancer. If you would like more information, contact the following agencies.

National Alliance of
Breast Cancer Organization (NABCO)
1180 Avenue of the Americas
2nd Floor
New York, NY 10036
(212) 719–0154

NABCO serves as a clearing house for breast cancer information. Membership in the group costs $25 per year and includes a subscription to their newsletter. They also publish an extensive resource list.

American Cancer Society (ACS)
1599 Clifton Road NE
Atlanta, GA 30329
(800) 227–2345

Listed below are the chartered divisions of the ACS.

Alabama Division, Inc.
402 Office Park Drive
Suite 300
Birmingham, Alabama 35223
(205) 879–2242

Alaska Division, Inc.
406 West Fireweed Lane
Suite 204
Anchorage, Alaska 99503
(907) 277–8696

Arizona Division, Inc.
2929 East Thomas Road
Phoenix, Arizona 85016
(602) 224–0524

Arkansas Division, Inc.
901 North University
Little Rock, Arkansas 77202
(501) 664–3480

California Division, Inc.
1710 Webster Street
P.O. Box 2061
Oakland, California 94612
(415) 893–7900

Colorado Division, Inc.
2255 South Oneida
P.O. Box 24669
Denver, Colorado 80224
(303) 758–2030

Connecticut Division, Inc.
Barnes Park South
14 Village Lane
Wallingford, Connecticut 06492
(203) 265–7161

Delaware Division, Inc.
92 Read's Way
New Castle, Delaware 19720
(302) 324–4227

District of Columbia Division, Inc.
1825 Connecticut Avenue, N.W.
Suite 315
Washington, D.C. 20009
(202) 483–2600

Florida Division, Inc.
1001 South MacDill Avenue
Tampa, Florida 33629
(813) 253–0541

Georgia Division, Inc.
46 Fifth Street, NE
Atlanta, Georgia 30308
(404) 892–0026

Hawaii/Pacific Division, Inc.
Community Services Center Bldg.
200 North Vineyard Boulevard
Honolulu, Hawaii 96817
(808) 531–1662

Idaho Division, Inc.
2676 Vista Avenue
P.O. Box 5386
Boise, Idaho 83705
(208) 343–4609

Illinois Division, Inc.
77 East Monroe
Chicago, Illinois 60603
(312) 641–6150

Indiana Division, Inc.
8730 Commerce Park Place
Indianapolis, Indiana 46268
(317) 872–4432

Iowa Division Inc.
8364 Hickman Road, Suite D
Des Moines, Iowa 50322
(515) 253–0147

Kansas Division, Inc.
1315 SW Arrowhead Road
Topeka, Kansas 66604
(913) 273–4114

Kentucky Division, Inc.
701 West Muhammed Ali Blvd.
P.O. Box 1807
Louisville, Kentucky 40217–1807
(502) 584–6782

Louisiana Division, Inc.
Fidelity Homestead Bldg.
837 Gravier Street
Suite 700
New Orleans, Louisiana 70112–1509
(504) 523–2029

Maine Division, Inc.
52 Federal Street
Brunswick, Maine 04011
(207) 729–3339

Maryland Division, Inc.
8219 Town Center Drive
P.O. Box 82
White Marsh, Maryland 21162–0082
(301) 529–7272

Massachusetts Division, Inc.
247 Commonwealth Avenue
Boston, Massachusetts 02116
(617) 267–2650

Michigan Division, Inc.
1205 East Saginaw Street
Lansing, Michigan 48906
(517) 371–2920

Minnesota Division, Inc.
3316 West 66th Street
Minneapolis, Minnesota 55435
(612) 925–2772

Mississippi Division, Inc.
1380 Livingston Lane
Lakeover Office Park
Jackson, Mississippi 39213
(601) 362–8874

Missouri Division, Inc.
3322 American Avenue
Jefferson City, Missouri 65102
(314) 893–4800

Montana Division, Inc.
313 N. 32nd Street
Suite #1
Billings, Montana 59101
(406) 252–7111

Nebraska Division, Inc.
8502 West Center Road
Omaha, Nebraska 68124–5255
(402) 393–5800

Nevada Division, Inc.
1325 East Harmon
Las Vegas, Nevada 89119
(702) 798–6857

New Hampshire Division, Inc.
360 Route 101, Unit 501
Bedford, New Hampshire 03102–
    6800
(603) 472–8899

New Jersey Division, Inc.
2600 Route 1, CNN 2201
North Brunswick, New Jersey 08902
(201) 297–8000

New Mexico Division, Inc.
5800 Lomas Blvd., N.E.
Albuquerque, New Mexico 87110
(505) 260–2105

New York State Division, Inc.
6725 Lyons Street
P.O. Box 7
East Syracuse, New York 13057
(315) 437–7025

  Long Island Division, Inc.
  145 Pidgeon Hill Road
  Huntington Station, New York
      11746
  (516) 385–9100

New York City Division, Inc.
19 West 56th Street
New York, New York 10019
(212) 586–8700

Queens Division, Inc.
112–25 Queens Boulevard
Forest Hills, New York 11375
(718) 263–2224

Westchester Division, Inc.
30 Glenn St.
White Plains, New York 10603
(914) 949–4800

North Carolina Division, Inc.
11 South Boylan Avenue
Suite 221
Raleigh, North Carolina 27603
(919) 834–8463

North Dakota Division, Inc.
123 Roberts Street
P.O. Box 426
Fargo, North Dakota 58107
(701) 232–1385

Ohio Division, Inc.
5555 Frantz Road
Dublin, Ohio 43017
(614) 889–9565

Oklahoma Division, Inc.
300 United Founders Blvd.
Suite 136
Oklahoma City, Oklahoma 73112
(405) 843–9888

Oregon Division, Inc.
0330 SW Curry
Portland, Oregon 97201
(503) 295–6422

Pennsylvania Division, Inc.
P.O. Box 897
Route 422 & Sipe Avenue
Hershey, Pennsylvania 17033–0897
(717) 533–6144

Philadelphia Division, Inc.
1422 Chestnut Street
Philadelphia, Pennsylvania 19102
(215) 665–2900

Puerto Rico Division, Inc.
Calle Alverio #577
Esquina Sargento Medina
Hato Rey, Puerto Rico 00918
(809) 764–2295

Rhode Island Division, Inc.
400 Main Street
Pawtucket, Rhode Island 02860
(401) 722–8480

South Carolina Division, Inc.
128 Stonemark Lane
Columbia, South Carolina 29210
(803) 750–1693

South Dakota Division, Inc.
4101 Carnegie Circle
Sioux Falls, South Dakota 57106–
2322
(605) 361–8277

Tennessee Division, Inc.
1315 Eighth Avenue, South
Nashville, Tennessee 37203
(615) 255–1ACS

Texas Division, Inc.
2433 Ridgepoint Drive
Austin, Texas 78754
(512) 928–2262

Utah Division, Inc.
610 East South Temple
Salt Lake City, Utah 84102
(801) 322–0431

Vermont Division, Inc.
13 Loomis Street, Drawer C
P.O. Box 1452
Montpelier, Vermont 05602–1452
(802) 223–2348

Virginia Division, Inc.
4240 Park Place Court
Glen Allen, Virginia 23060
(804) 270–0142/(800) ACS–2345

Wisconsin Division, Inc.
615 North Sherman Avenue
Madison, Wisconsin 53704
(608) 249–0487

Washington Division, Inc.
2120 First Avenue North
Seattle, Washington 98109–1140
(206) 283–1152

Wyoming Division, Inc.
2222 House Avenue
Cheyenne, Wyoming 82001
(307) 638–3331

West Virginia Division, Inc.
2428 Kanawha Boulevard
East Charleston, West Virginia 25311
(304) 344–3611

Canadians can contact:
Canadian Cancer Society
77 Bloor Street, Suite 1702
Toronto, Ontario M5S3A1
(416) 961–7223

Reach to Recovery. This supportive arm of the American Cancer Society recruits its volunteers from women who have themselves suffered breast cancer. These wonderful women can be a source of comfort, information, and support at a time when you may feel at your lowest ebb. They have been in your position; they have known the fears, the anger, the frustration, and the pain of having a breast removed. All you need to do is ask them, and they will be only too glad to share their knowledge and experience with you or to serve as a sounding board against which you can ventilate your own feelings and help you to adjust emotionally and physically. You can contact a Reach to Recovery volunteer through your local American Cancer Society.

ENCORE. ENCORE stands for Encouragement, Normalcy, Counseling, Opportunity, Reach Out, Energies revived and is sponsored by the national YWCA. This program for postoperative breast cancer patients includes exercise sessions to music, exercise sessions in water, and group discussion periods. It is designed to assist you in physical recovery in an atmosphere of warmth and emotional support and to put you in touch with other women in your position. In some areas, the program runs continuously; however, in other locations, it may only be offered when needed. Check the YWCA nearest you for more information.

Breast Reconstruction

For questions about the procedure and for help in finding a certified plastic surgeon in your area, contact

The American Society of Plastic and Reconstructive Surgeons
Suite 1900
233 North Michigan Avenue
Chicago, IL 60601

or call the twenty-four-hour patient referral service at (312) 856–1818.

Physicians Data Query

This computerized data base of the National Cancer Institute offers the most up-to-date information about new treatments for many types of cancer, clinical trials available to patients, and organizations involved in caring for cancer patients. For information on how you or your physician can get access to PDQ, call the Cancer Information Service at (800) 4–CANCER.

For information on support groups or organizations to assist patients and their families in home care, contact the Cancer Care Foundation at (800) 282–2873, the American Cancer Society national headquarters, or your local American Cancer Society chapter and ask for a Reach To Recovery volunteer (see the listing of ACS divisions earlier in this chapter).

Guided Imagery

Direct inquiries concerning this technique should go to:

Health Training and Research Center
P.O. Box 7237
Little Rock, AR 72217–7237
(501) 224–1933

The center provides training programs for professionals, education courses for patients and their families, an international directory of professionals trained in the Simonton approach method, and consultation to medical and psychological facilities wishing to establish their own programs.

Supplemental Reading Sources for Guided Imagery

Joan Borysenko, *Minding the Body, Mending the Mind* (New York: Bantam Books, 1988).

Kenneth R. Pelletier, *Mind as Healer, Mind as Slayer* (New York: Dell, 1977).

Norman Cousins, *Anatomy of an Illness* (New York: Bantam Books, 1982).

Bernard Siegel, *Love, Medicine, and Miracles* (New York: Harper & Row, 1988).

Bernard Siegel, *Peace, Love, and Healing* (New York: Harper & Row, 1989).

Carl Simonton, et al., *Getting Well Again* (New York: Bantam Books, 1982).

Adelaide Bry and Marjorie Bair, *Directing the Movies of the Mind: Visualization for Health and Insight* (New York: Harper & Row, 1978).

A listing of related audiocassettes is available through the Health Training and Research Center at the above address.

Nutritional Information

Information about Omega-3 Fatty Acids
Direct product information questions to:

BioSyn Corporation
21 Tioga Way
Marblehead, MA 01945

Supplemental Reading on Diet, Fatty Acids, and Nutrition
Julius Fast, *The Omega-3 Breakthrough* (Tucson: The Body Press, 1987). This book provides a clear overview of omega-3 oil benefits—particularly how fish oils lower levels of cholesterol and triglycerides—and may thus provide a preventive tune-up against heart disease. Interviews with medical specialists explore how fish oil helps prevent blood clots and can reduce cancer risk factors.

Laura J. Stevens, *The New Way to Sugar Free Recipes* (New York: Doubleday). This book includes 125 sugar-free, lower calorie recipes for many foods ranging from jams to pies and cakes.

Francyne Davis, *The Low Blood Sugar Cookbook* (New York: Bantam Books, 1985 rev. ed.). This cookbook contains more than 250 low-sugar and low-starch recipes that prove that reducing sugar doesn't mean giving up taste.

Michael R. Eades, *Thin So Fast* (New York: Warner Books, 1989). All right, let me fess up right at the outset and admit to you that this is indeed the same Michael R. Eades who is my husband. And that fact cannot help but make me a somewhat biased reviewer of this diet and health book. However, and I truly mean this, it has been called by both physicians and research experts who don't happen to be his spouse "a book offering the best and most concise dietary information available" and "the nutritional text for the remainder of the century."

John Yudkin, *Sweet and Dangerous* (New York: Bantam Books, 1972). Although not a cookbook, it is a must-read book for anyone concerned about the many serious threats to health that a high sugar intake can cause. You may want to read this one to convince yourself that giving up excess sugar really is in your best interest.

Experts now believe that reducing sugar intake is an important part of reducing your breast cancer risk, and this may entail some changes in your style of cooking. Because diabetic patients have been faced with this same problem (reducing sugar intake) for years, there are a great many cookbooks geared to helping the diabetic patient with cooking. Although you may not be diabetic, don't hesitate to check out these cookbooks; they will often prove to be veritable gold mines of lower-sugar recipes that you may enjoy. I have listed a few of these for you to get you started.

Mary Jane Finsand, *Diabetic Snack and Appetizer Cookbook* (New York: Sterling Publishing, 1987). This book gives hundreds of delicious and healthy snacks low in sugar.

Katharine Middleton and Marry Abbott Hess, *The Art of Cooking for the Diabetic* (Chicago: Contemporary Books, 1978). This cookbook will give you more than 300 recipes to take you from soup to nuts while keeping sugar intake low.

Body Fat Calculation Tables

You can find instructions to calculate your own percent body fat in either of these books.

Michael R. Eades, *Thin So Fast* (New York: Warner Books, 1989).

Dennis Remington, Garth Fisher, and Edward Parent, *How to Lower Your Fat Thermostat* (Provo: Vitality Press, 1983).

Recommended Daily Allowances

Table 3 lists the U.S. Recommended Daily Allowances compiled by the Food and Nutrition Board of the National Academy of Sciences and the National Research Council.

Stop Smoking Regimens

A number of effective programs in community hospitals, medical centers, and private clinics to treat smoking addiction have opened in recent years, using every method of treatment from behavior modification, to aversion therapy, to hypnosis.

In the stop smoking program we run through our practice, we have used several methods that seem to work. Let your doctor decide if any of the following treatments might work for you.

Catapres TSS Patches. These patches seem to reduce the nicotine craving. Smokers generally must use the patches for three or four weeks while they try to quit. (This is a prescription drug.)

Doxepin (Adapin) at Bedtime. This antidepressant drug is administered in gradually increasing doses over the course of a few weeks. Once at the upper-limit dose, the patient should make the commitment to stop smoking and should find the expected anxiety and withdrawal much less uncomfortable. The drug is

Table 3. Recommended Dietary Allowances,[a] Revised 1989
(Designed for the maintenance of good nutrition of practically all healthy people in the United States)

Category	Age (years) or Condition	Weight[b] (kg)	Weight[b] (lb)	Height[b] (cm)	Height[b] (in)	Protein (g)	Fat-Soluble Vitamins Vitamin A (mg RE)[c]	Vitamin D (mg)[d]	Vitamin E (mg a-TE)[c]	Vitamin K (mg)
Infants	0.0–0.5	6	13	60	24	13	375	7.5	3	5
	0.5–1.0	9	20	71	28	14	375	10	4	10
Children	1–3	13	29	90	35	16	400	10	6	15
	4–6	20	44	112	44	24	500	10	7	20
	7–10	28	62	132	52	28	700	10	7	30
Males	11–14	45	99	157	62	45	1,000	10	10	45
	15–18	66	145	176	69	59	1,000	10	10	65
	19–24	72	160	177	70	58	1,000	10	10	70
	25–50	79	174	176	70	63	1,000	5	10	80
	51+	77	170	173	68	63	1,000	5	10	80
Females	11–14	46	101	157	62	46	800	10	8	45
	15–18	55	120	163	64	44	800	10	8	55
	19–24	58	128	164	65	46	800	10	8	60
	25–50	63	138	163	64	50	800	5	8	65
	51+	65	143	160	63	50	800	5	8	65
Pregnant						60	800	10	10	65
Lactating	1st 6 months					65	1,300	10	12	65
	2nd 6 months					62	1,200	10	11	65

[a]The allowances, expressed as average daily intakes over time, are intended to provide for individual variations among most normal persons as they live in the United States under usual environmental stresses. Diets should be based on a variety of common foods to provide other nutrients for which human requirements have been less well defined.
[b]Weights and heights of reference adults are actual medians for the U.S. population of the designated age, as reported by a National Health and Nutrition Examination Survey (NHANES II). The median weights and heights of those under nineteen years of age were taken from the *American Journal of Clinical Nutrition*, 32:602–629, Hamill et al. (1979). The use of these figures does not imply that the height-to-weight ratios are ideal.

Table 3 (continued).

	Water-Soluble Vitamins							Minerals						
Category	Vita-min C (mg)	Thia-min (mg)	Ribo-flavin (mg)	Niacin (mg NE)f	Vita-min B6 (mg)	Fo-late (mg)	Vita-min B12 (mg)	Cal-cium (mg)	Phos-phorus (mg)	Mag-nesium (mg)	Iron (mg)	Zinc (mg)	Iodine (mg)	Sele-nium (mg)
Infants	30	0.3	0.4	5	0.3	25	0.3	400	300	40	6	5	40	10
	35	0.4	0.5	6	0.6	35	0.5	600	500	60	10	5	50	15
Children	40	0.7	0.8	9	1.0	50	0.7	800	800	80	10	10	70	20
	45	0.9	1.1	12	1.1	75	1.0	800	800	120	10	10	90	20
	45	1.0	1.2	13	1.4	100	1.4	800	800	170	10	10	120	30
Males	50	1.3	1.5	17	1.7	150	2.0	1,200	1,200	270	12	15	150	40
	60	1.5	1.8	20	2.0	200	2.0	1,200	1,200	400	12	15	150	50
	60	1.5	1.7	19	2.0	200	2.0	1,200	1,200	350	10	15	150	70
	60	1.5	1.7	19	2.0	200	2.0	800	800	350	10	15	150	70
	60	1.2	1.4	15	2.0	200	2.0	800	800	350	10	15	150	70
Females	50	1.1	1.3	15	1.4	150	2.0	1,200	1,200	280	15	12	150	45
	60	1.1	1.3	15	1.5	180	2.0	1,200	1,200	300	15	12	150	50
	60	1.1	1.3	15	1.6	180	2.0	1,200	1,200	280	15	12	150	55
	60	1.0	1.2	13	1.6	180	2.0	800	800	280	15	12	150	55
	60	1.0	1.2	13	1.6	180	2.0	800	800	280	10	12	150	55
Pregnant	70	1.5	1.6	17	2.2	400	2.2	1,200	1,200	320	30	15	175	65
Lactating	95	1.6	1.8	20	2.1	280	2.6	1,200	1,200	355	15	19	200	75
	90	1.6	1.7	20	2.1	260	2.6	1,200	1,200	340	15	16	200	75

c Retinol equivalents. 1 retinol equivalent = 1 mg retinol or 6 mg b-carotene.
d As cholecalciferol. 10 mg cholecalciferol = 400 IU of vitamin D.
e a-Tocopherol equivalents. 1 mg d-a tocopherol = 1 a-TE.
f NE (niacin equivalent) is equal to 1 mg of niacin or 60 mg of dietary tryptophan.

Recommended Dietary Allowances, © 1989 by the National Academy of Sciences, National Academy Press, Washington, DC.

taken for several weeks after smoking is stopped and then slowly discontinued. (This is a prescription drug.)

Sphenopalatine Ganglion Block.   Lidocaine, a local anaesthetic, is applied topically through the nose to prevent symptoms of withdrawal from nicotine. Once the commitment to quit has been made, the patient must undergo treatment for twenty minutes on five consecutive days. He or she must not smoke or chew Nicorette gum, because that defeats the purpose of the procedure—blocking withdrawal symptoms. We use this as only part of a program combining group counseling, Catapres TSS patches, and a mild anxiolytic. If your doctors would like more information about our program, please have them write to our clinic:

Medi-Stat Medical Clinic
8116 Cantrell Road
Little Rock, AR 72207

Your local chapter of the American Cancer Society, the American Heart Association, or the American Lung Association can provide more information on how to quit smoking.

Glossary

Antiestrogen drugs. Medications used in treatment of cancers (such as some breast cancers) that are sensitive to or grow in response to the effects of estrogen and progestin hormones. These drugs work against the cancer by blocking the effect of the hormones or lowering their levels in the blood.

Benign. Not harmful, mild, not malignant.

Carcinogen. A substance (such as a chemical) that can cause cancer to develop.

Chromosomes. The microscopic rod-shaped collections of genetic material in the nucleus of each cell that direct its activity. Humans have twenty-three pairs of chromosomes in each normal cell.

Doppler flow study. A diagnostic test that measures blood flow to or through an organ, blood vessel, or other area based on differences in the level of sound generated by the passage of blood during each heartbeat as compared to between beats. Obstetricians use this same kind of machine to hear the baby's heartbeat long before it can be heard with the normal stethoscope.

Environment. The surroundings, conditions, and external factors that affect us.

Estrogen. A female sex, or reproductive, hormone produced primarily by the ovaries.

Estrogen replacement drug. Natural or synthetic (artificial) estrogen compounds taken orally, by injection, or absorbed through the skin from patches to replace the hormone after loss of ovary function through menopause or surgery.

Fibroadenoma. A solid, rubbery breast lump composed of fibrous connective (supportive) tissue and glandular lining tissues. These lumps are usually benign.

Fibrocyst. A knotty-feeling breast tissue lump that is composed of fibrous connective (supportive) tissue and fluid-filled sacklike interspaces called cysts. These lumps are usually benign.

First-degree relative. Those direct, biological relatives of the same generation or one removed, i.e., your biological parents, full sisters or brothers, and your own children.

Genes. The basic units of heredity found in predictable constant locations on the chromosomes.

Genetics. The study of heredity.

Heredity. The capacity to develop traits and characteristics possessed by one's ancestors, which are dependent on the chromosomes from which one develops.

Lymph. The colorless fluid that bathes the tissues of the body.

Lymph gland or node. A rounded beanlike swelling of specialized immune tissue that produces certain types of white blood cell (a part of the immune system) and filters out impurities such as bacteria or cancer cells. These glands are scattered throughout the body, but collect in groups especially prominent in the neck, under the arm, and in the groin.

Malignant. Harmful, resisting treatment, tending or threatening to cause death.

Mammogram. A special X ray of the breast used to detect or evaluate breast lumps and cancers.

Menopause. The time in a woman's life that marks the permanent cessation of her menstrual activity.

Monounsaturated fats. Such oils as olive and canola (or rapeseed) oils that contain only one double bond (see *Saturated fats*). Consumption of these oils has been associated with lower breast cancer and heart disease risk.

Obesity. The condition of excess body weight 30 to 40 percent above ideal for height and frame size, or more specifically having a percentage of body fat greater than 30 percent of total weight.

Omega-3 fatty acid. An essential dietary polyunsaturated fat with a number of anti-inflammatory and blood-thinning properties. It is found primarily in the fat of cold-water fish (tuna, mackerel, salmon, herring, etc.).

Pap smear. A test that samples (by softly scraping) cells of the cervix of the uterus. The pathologist then microscopically examines the samples, after they have been placed on a glass slide and stained, to detect cervical cancer and the effect of certain viruses.

Polyunsaturated fats. Fats (usually from vegetable sources such as corn, safflower, peanut, etc.) that are liquids—or oils—at room temperature because their chemical structure is not as stable as saturated fats (see *Saturated fats*). People seeking to reduce the amount of harmful fat in their diet should reduce saturated fat intake in favor of polyunsaturated fats.

Postmenopausal breast cancer. The most frequently occurring type of breast cancer, which occurs after a woman has reached menopause.

Precancerous lump. A breast tissue growth that under microscopic examination does not appear entirely normal, but that has not yet developed those characteristics that would mark it as malignant or cancerous. It may represent a step along the way to a cancer.

Premenopausal breast cancer. The type of breast cancer that occurs during a woman's early life when she still has active menstrual cycles (i.e., before menopause). This kind of cancer displays a strong tendency to run in the family.

Saturated fats. Those fats that are solid at room temperature, such as butter, lard, animal fats, and some of the tropical plant oils such as coconut and palm oils. All fats and oils are composed of chains of carbon atoms joined together in chemical bonds. "Saturated" means that in the fat molecule in every possible bonding spot at which the carbon atoms could be bonded chemically to a hydrogen, they have been. Consumption of saturated fats can raise blood cholesterol.

Tamoxifen. The chemical name for the most commonly used antiestrogen drug.

Tumor. A new growth of tissue forming a mass that has no physiologic function and that may not be restricted by the normal laws of growth.

Ultrasound. A diagnostic test that uses sound waves, bounced off internal organs or suspected masses, to produce a characteristic "echo" pattern that outlines the organ or mass in question. The process is much like sonar on a submarine. The ultrasound can show the radiologist whether a lump in the breast is a fluid-filled cyst or a solid tumor.

Xeromammogram. Another kind of special X-ray examination of the breast that may be slightly more sensitive in detecting breast cancers than a standard mammography, but which requires more radiation.

Index

About the Authors

Dr. Mary Dan Eades was born and raised in Arkansas, where she attended the University of Arkansas, graduating magna cum laude. In 1981 she received her M.D. from the University's School of Medical Science. In 1982, together with her husband, Michael Eades, M.D., Dr. Eades opened the first in a chain of Medi-Stat clinics that specialize in family medicine. Dr. Eades makes her home in Little Rock with her husband and her three beautiful sons, Ted, Daniel and Scott.

Dr. Attila Toth is presently Associate Professor of Obstetrics and Gynecology, Cornell University Medical College; Director of the MacLeod Laboratory for Infertility; and Attending Physician, The New York Hospital. He is a member of the American Fertility Society, the American Society of Andrology, the American Society of Reproductive Immunology, and the New York Obstetrical Society and the author of over 50 scientific publications.

C. Scott McMillin is the director of the Suburban Hospital Addiction Treatment Center and an adjunct faculty member at the University of Virginia. He is the co-author of numerous books, including *Don't Help: A Positive Guide to Working with the Alcoholic* and *The Twelve Steps Revisited*.